FINISH LINE

Writing

for the Common Core State Standards

Continental

Acknowledgments

Illustrations: Page 27, 164, 176 *map,* 183, 192 *runners*: Laurie Conley; Page 34: Harry Norcross; Page 149 *street map:* Doris Ettlinger; Page 192 *skiers:* Margaret Lindmark

Photographs: Page 7: www.photos.com; Page 26: www.photos.com; Page 39: Siede Preis; Page 58: C Squared Studios; Page 73: www.photos.com; Page 93: www.photos.com; Page 103: www.istockphoto.com/Hugh Stonelan; Page 118: PhotoLink; Page 124: Scott T. Baxter; Page 133: C Squared Studios; Page 139: Image used under Creative Commons from Nevit Dilmen; Page 168: www.istockphoto.com/cpaquin; Page 175 *bear* www.photos.com, *tracks* www.istockphoto.com/Natural_warp

ISBN 978-0-8454-6951-4

Copyright © 2011 The Continental Press, Inc.

Table of Contents

Welcome to Finish Line Writing for the Common Core State Standards

This book will help you become a good writer. It will also help you get ready for writing tests.

The lessons in this book follow the Common Core State Standards for English Language Arts and Literacy in History, Social Studies, Science, and Technical Subjects. The Common Core State Standards (CCSS) build on the education standards developed by the states. This book will help you practice the writing skills you need.

In the lessons of this book, you will review the writing process. Then you will use those skills in different types of writing. You will also read informational text and stories. Then you will answer multiple-choice and writing questions about them. The lessons are in three parts:

- The first part talks about the writing skill you are going to study and explains what it is and how you use it.

- The second part is called Guided Practice. You will get more than practice here; you will get help. You will read a nonfiction passage and answer questions about it. After each question, the correct answer will be explained or a sample answer will be given. So you will answer questions and find out right away if you were correct.

- The third part is Test Yourself. Here you will read a question and then write an answer on your own.

After you have finished all of the lessons and units, you will take a Practice Test at the end of the book.

Now you are ready to begin using this book. Good luck!

You know what writing is. You know there are different kinds of writing. This unit tells about writing.

- **Lesson 1** is about the writing steps. There are five steps. You use these every time you write.

- **Lesson 2** tells about paragraphs. You will find out what makes a good paragraph.

- **Lesson 3** is about the main idea. It is also about the details. The details help explain the main idea.

- **Lesson 4** tells about cause and effect. This kind of writing tells what happened. It also tells why it happened.

- **In Lesson 5,** you'll learn to write about how two things are alike. You'll also learn to write about how they are not alike.

The Writing Process

W.1.2, 3, 5, 6

Writing is a process. It takes a number of steps. Most writers follow these five steps:

Prewriting → Drafting → Revising → Editing → Publishing

Here is an easy way to remember the writing process. First, you **plan** what you will write. This step is prewriting. Next, you **write.** This step is drafting. Then you go back and **change** your writing. This step is revising. In the last step, you **check,** or edit, your work. This means you proofread. You fix mistakes in spelling and punctuation. Finally, you publish, or **show,** your writing.

Step 1: Prewriting

Prewriting is planning. In this step, you plan what you will write. You need to answer these questions:

Read
Note
Organize

- Who will read it? This is your **audience.**
- What will you write about? This is your **subject.**
- Why are you writing? This is your **purpose.**
- What will you say? This is your **content.**
- How will you say it? This is your **voice.**

Sometimes, you are writing for a test. The test question will tell you these things. Here is a question from a test.

> There are many kinds of bears. Write a story for your teacher. Write about the panda bear and the polar bear. Show how they are the same. Show how they are different. Be sure to:
> - tell how they are different
> - tell how they are alike

The clue words tell you what to do.
- You will **write a story.**
- The **subject** is the polar bear and the panda bear.
- The **purpose** is to show how two things are alike. It is also to show how they are different.
- The **audience** is your teacher.

The rest is up to you. You need to think about what you will say. You are telling how the bears are alike. Make notes about what you will write.

Read
Note
Organize

A chart will help you know what to write. It helps you put your ideas together. A Venn diagram will help answer this question. You can write down what you know about each thing. Write down what is the same. Then write down what is different. Here is the chart Evan used.

Read
Note
Organize

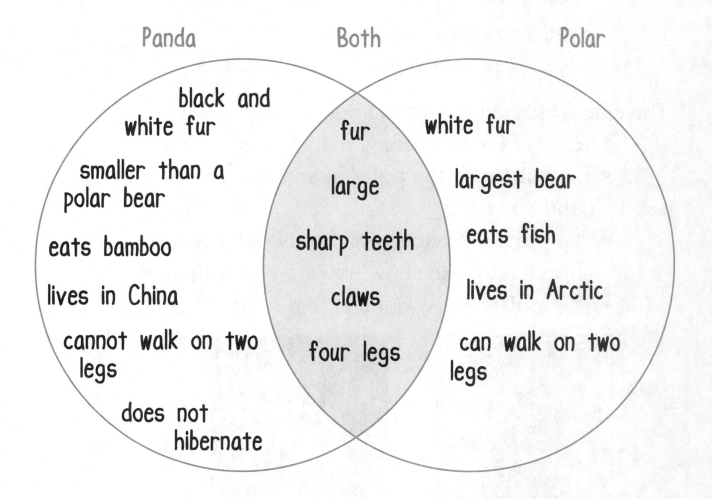

Panda | Both | Polar

Panda:
- black and white fur
- smaller than a polar bear
- eats bamboo
- lives in China
- cannot walk on two legs
- does not hibernate

Both:
- fur
- large
- sharp teeth
- claws
- four legs

Polar:
- white fur
- largest bear
- eats fish
- lives in Arctic
- can walk on two legs

Guided Practice

> The class is putting on a play. The teacher asks the students to write a letter to their parents. The letter will tell about the holiday play. It must give facts about the play. The play is a story the class wrote. Be sure to:
> - tell the date and the place
> - tell other facts about the play

Who is the audience?

  A classmates

  B teacher

  C parents

  D principal

You are writing for your parents. Choice C is the correct answer. The teacher gave the assignment. Your classmates are writing letters, too. The principal will not read the letter. Choices A, B, and D are incorrect.

Which word in the question would you underline to help you know what to write?

  A play

  B facts

  C story

  D letter

 You are writing a letter. Choice D is the correct answer. You are writing about the play. The play is a story the class wrote. You will give facts in the letter. Choices A, B, and C are incorrect.

Step 2: Drafting

You planned what you would write in the first step. The next step is to write. You think about your main idea. Then you think about facts that support the main idea. This step is called **drafting.**

Here is what Evan wrote about the two bears. He used the ideas from his Venn diagram. He told his main idea. Then he used details to support it. He also used connecting words.

The polar bear and the panda bear are alike in some ways. But they are different, two. Both bears have claws and fur. However, their fur is not the same color. The polar bear has white fur. This is because it lives in the Arctic. It is snowy there. The polar bear's fru helps it blend in. The panda bear is black and white. It lives in the mountains of china. Both bears are large. The polar bear is larger than the panda. It can walk on its two legs. The panda bear cannot walk on its two legs. These bears do not hibernate like other bears.

Step 3: Revising

You are finished writing. Now, you will make changes to make your writing better. This is called **revising.** Ask yourself these questions. Your answers will help you think about changes you should make.

- Do I have a main idea?
- Do I need to add any details?
- Do I need to take out any details that are not important?
- Does my writing have a beginning, a middle, and an end?
- Are my ideas clear?
- Are my sentences well written?

GUIDED PRACTICE

Read Evan's revised story. Look for changes. Then answer the questions.

The polar bear and the panda bear are alike in some ways. But they are different, two. Both bears have claws and fur. However, their fur is not the same color. The polar bear has white fur. This is because it lives in the Arctic. It is snowy there. The polar bear's fru helps it blend in. The panda bear is black and white. It lives in the mountains of china. Both bears are large. The polar bear is larger than the panda. It can walk on its two back legs. The panda bear cannot walk on its two legs. These bears do not hibernate like other bears. The polar bear and panda bear are interesting bears.

Why did Evan add the last sentence?

A The paragraph needed an introduction.

B The paragraph needed more facts.

C The paragraph needed to be longer.

D The paragraph needed a conclusion.

The last sentence sums up the main idea in the paragraph. Choice D is the correct answer. Choice A is incorrect. The paragraph has an introduction. Choice B is incorrect. This sentence does not add any facts. It is an opinion. Choice C is incorrect. The paragraph does not have to be a certain length.

Write a title for the story.

_____

_____

The title tells about the main idea of a story. Here is an example:

Polar Bears and Panda Bears

Why did the writer add the word <u>back</u>?

_____

_____

 The writer adds words or sentences to make his meaning clear. Here is a sample answer:

He wanted to tell which legs the polar bear can walk on.

Peer Review

The teacher may have students edit each other's papers. This is called **peer review.** Students work in pairs. They use a checklist to edit each other's papers. This list tells what a writer has to do to get a good score. It tells what the paper must have to win this score. An example of a checklist is given on page 16.

Checklist for Writing Alike and Different

Score 3
- The writing answers all parts of the question.
- The writing shows two ways the subjects are alike.
- The writing shows two ways the subjects are different.
- The writer uses connecting words.
- There are many good supporting details.
- Capitalization and punctuation are correct.

Score 2
- The writing answers almost all parts of the question.
- The writing shows one way the subjects are alike.
- The writing shows one way the subjects are different.
- The writer uses some connecting words.
- There are some supporting details.
- There are some mistakes in capitalization and punctuation.

Score 1
- The writing answers only part of the question.
- The writing does not show ways the subjects are alike.
- The writing does not show ways the subjects are different.
- The writer uses few or no connecting words.
- There are not many supporting details.
- There are many mistakes in capitalization and punctuation.

Step 4: Editing

You are finished revising. Now, you will make little changes to make your writing better. This step is called **editing.** You will make sure that:

- All words are spelled correctly.
- You've used capital letters correctly.
- You've used the right punctuation marks.
- Subjects and verbs go together.

Go over your writing sentence by sentence and word by word. Mark the places that need to be corrected. This is called **proofreading.** When you proofread, you use these marks to show where changes can be made.

Proofreading Symbols	
∧ Add letters or words.	Our flag now has 50 ∧ stars.
⊙ Add a period.	We salute our flag ⊙
≡ Capitalize a letter.	The united states flag has changed.
∧ Add a comma.	Our country's flag is red, white ∧ and blue.
ℐ Delete letters or words.	The flag has 13 stripes stripes.
∿ Switch the position of letters or words.	One was star added for each state.

Practice using proofreading marks with this paragraph.

Our country's falg has changed many times. It had only 13 stars and stripes at first? Then new States joined the union. So, more stars and stripes were added. Soon, there were many states. It was decided to add only a star for each new state. There would only be 13 stripes, one stripe for each of the original states. Our flag now has 50 stars. How many states do we have! How many original states were there?

Were you able to find all the mistakes? Here are the corrections:

Sentence 1: Change falg to flag.

Sentence 2: Change the question mark to a period.

Sentence 3: Change States to states.

Sentence 10: Change the exclamation point to a question mark.

Look at the draft below. It has proofreading corrections. Can you identify them? Circle the corrected mistakes you see.

The polar bear and the panda bear are alike in some ways. But they are different, ~~two~~ too. Both bears have claws and fur. However, their fur is not the same color. The polar bear has white fur. This is because it lives in the Arctic. It is snowy there. The polar bear's fru helps it blend in. The panda bear is black and white. It lives in the mountains of china. Both bears are large. The polar bear is larger than the panda. It can walk on its two back legs. The panda bear cannot walk on its two legs. These bears do not hibernate like other bears. The polar bear and panda bear are interesting bears.

✔ **Did you find the mistakes? Here are the correct answers:**

Mistake 1: Change two to the word too in sentence 1.
Mistake 2: Change fru to fur in sentence 6.
Mistake 3: Capitalize China in sentence 8.

Step 5: Publishing

Now, you are ready to share your writing. This is called **publishing.** This is the last step. You can do this many ways. You can turn in your paper to your teacher. You can read it to your class. Your teacher might have you make a poster. Or, you can make a slide show. Publishing can take many forms.

Test Yourself

There are many kinds of sports. Some need many players to play. Some only need one person. Write a paragraph about two sports. Tell how the two sports are the same. Then tell how they are different. Be sure to:

- use a topic sentence
- tell how they are the same
- tell how they are different

1 What are you asked to write about?

Read
Note
Organize

_____

_____

_____

_____

_____

2 Use this Venn diagram to plan your answer.

Sport 1   Both   Sport 2

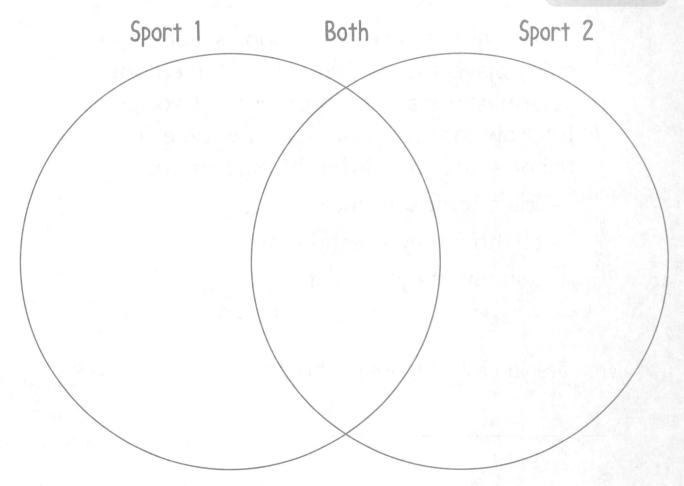

UNIT 1 ▨▨▨▨▨▨▨▨▨▨▨▨▨▨▨▨▨▨▨▨▨▨▨▨▨▨▨▨▨▨▨▨▨▨
Elements of Writing

3 Now, write your answer to the question. Use your planner to help you answer the question.

_____

_____

_____

_____

_____

_____

_____

_____

_____

_____

_____

4 Reread what you have written. Is your main idea clear? Are your sentences well written? Read your work again. Be sure that you have spelled all the words right. Use the checklist on page 16 to check your writing. Have a classmate edit your writing if necessary.

_____

_____

_____

_____

_____

_____

_____

_____

_____

_____

_____

5 When you are happy with your work, copy it carefully on the lines below. Then publish your work by showing it to your teacher.

_____

_____

_____

_____

_____

_____

_____

_____

_____

_____

_____

Writing a Paragraph

W.1.2, 5, 6

A paragraph is about one idea. This is called the **main idea.** The **topic sentence** tells the main idea. Most times it is the first sentence of the paragraph. Sometimes, it may come later. All the other sentences tell about the main idea. They give **details** or facts.

Guided Practice

Read the paragraphs. Then answer the questions.

Snow

Snow is made from water in the clouds. First, the water collects in clouds. The water turns to ice when the air gets very cold. Finally, it falls to the ground. By the time it reaches the roads, it becomes snow.

Which is the topic sentence in the paragraph?

A sentence 1

B sentence 2

C sentence 3

D sentence 4

The topic sentence tells what the paragraph is about. It can be any sentence in the paragraph. However, most times it is the first sentence. Choice A is the correct answer. The first sentence tells what snow is. The other sentences give more facts about snow. Choices B, C, and D are incorrect.

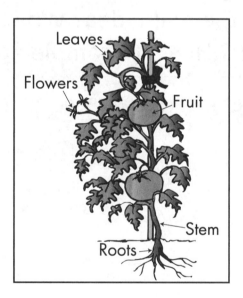

Topic: Tomatoes

_____

_____

Most people think that a tomato is a vegetable. But a tomato is more like an apple or an orange. It is a fruit. A fruit holds the parts of the plant that will make new plants. It has seeds inside. The ones in a tomato are small and yellow. Most fruit grows on trees that live a long time. Tomatoes grow on plants. They die each year. New seeds need to be put in the ground to get more.

Write a topic sentence for the paragraph.

_____

_____

 First, read the paragraph. Then think about the subject. What is the main idea? What is the subject of the paragraph? Here is a sample answer:

Is the tomato a vegetable or a fruit?

Organizing the Paragraph

Every sentence in a paragraph should be about the subject. This chart shows the order of the sentences in the paragraph about snow on page 26.

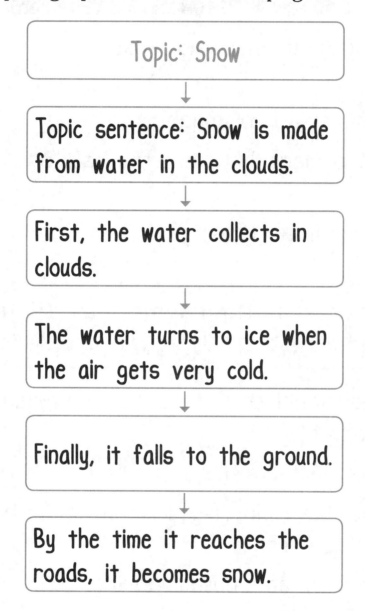

Topic: Snow

↓

Topic sentence: Snow is made from water in the clouds.

↓

First, the water collects in clouds.

↓

The water turns to ice when the air gets very cold.

↓

Finally, it falls to the ground.

↓

By the time it reaches the roads, it becomes snow.

A paragraph should end with a **closing sentence.** This sentence sums up the paragraph. The closing sentence in the paragraph on page 26 is "By the time it reaches the roads, it becomes snow."

Guided Practice

Read the sentences. Tell which is the topic sentence. Then number the sentences in order. Use them to write a paragraph. Add a closing sentence.

_____ They are black in the back and white in the front.

_____ This lets them stand up straight.

_____ They have short legs that are set far back on their bodies.

_____ Penguins are unusual looking.

✓ **Tell the main idea. Then number the sentences in the order you use them. Here is a sample answer:**

__2__ They are black in the back and white in the front.

__4__ This lets them stand up straight.

__3__ They have short legs that are set far back on their bodies.

__1__ Penguins are unusual looking.

Penguins are unusual looking. They are black in the back and white in the front. They have short legs that are set far back on their bodies. This lets them stand up straight. Penguins don't look like any other bird.

There are many ways to set up a paragraph. Which order will you choose? It depends on the kind of writing you are doing. Here are some ways to put information in order.

Sometimes, you write a paragraph to explain something. You can do this in two ways. You can give **details** that support your main idea. The paragraph on snow gives this kind of detail. The second way is to give **examples** of the main idea.

You use **time order** when you write a story. You need to tell the events in the order that they happened. Connecting words and phrases help you put things in time order. Use words such as first, then, after that, later, and finally.

Use **location** when you are describing a scene. Explain where things are in your description. If you want to describe a new park, you might use connecting words and phrases, such as close by, far away, or around.

Look at these words and phrases. They can help you describe a scene or location.

across	beside	close by	next to
behind	between	near	in front of

Guided Practice

Read the question. Then write a response.

Think about your lunchroom. Where do you sit? Who or what is near you? Write a short paragraph describing where you sit in your classroom. Use the words on page 31 to help you write your paragraph.

_____

_____

_____

_____

 This question asks you to use location to tell what you see. Explain clearly where things are in your description. This helps the reader see what you see. Here is a sample answer:

The lunchroom has two very long tables. I sit at the end of the second one. It is the table closest to the lunch line. We sit in the same place every day. Sara sits across from me. Devon sits next to me.

Writing for a Test

Sometimes, you must write a short answer to answer a question on a test. Your answer should be a paragraph. Use these steps to write your answer in the time you are given.

1. Underline the key words. This will help you understand the question.
2. Think about what you want to say.
3. Decide which plan you will use to set up your paragraph.
4. Write your topic sentence first. Then finish your paragraph.
5. Check your answer. You can still make changes.

Guided Practice

Read this article about cowboys. Then read the test question.

Cowboys

Most people know what a cowboy is. On TV shows, these ranch workers seem to have exciting lives. But their lives were not what you might think. A cowboy's job was lonely. He might see only one or two other cowboys for weeks. His job was full of hard work.

Taking care of cattle was not easy. The cows often got stuck in mud or wire. Sometimes, they got sick.

The best part of a cowboy's year was roundup time. This was held in the fall and spring. All of the cattle were gathered together. The new calves were marked. Each got the ranch owner's sign. This sign was called a brand. It showed everyone who owned the calves.

After roundup, cowboys from different ranches had contests. They tested one another to see who was best. They might rope cattle. Or, they might break wild horses. These contests became today's rodeos.

Would you have liked to be a cowboy? Write a paragraph telling why or why not. Use details from the passage to help you. In your answer, be sure to:

- include a topic sentence stating your main idea
- give details that explain your opinion

Here is how Antonio wrote his answer. First, he underlined important parts of the question. Then he made some notes. He knew he would need to write about his own opinion. He planned to use main idea and details for his paragraph.

Read
Note
Organize

To plan his writing, Antonio wrote down his main idea. Then he listed reasons. Here is what he wrote:

My Opinion: No, I would not have liked to be a cowboy.
Reason/Fact 1: I do not like to be outdoors in bad weather.
Reason/Fact 2: I like being around my family and friends.
Reason/Fact 3: Cowboys had to be good with animals.

Antonio finished his plan. Then he used his plan to write his paragraph.

I would not have wanted to be a cowboy. I enjoy being outdoors. But I do not like to be outside in bad weather. Cowboys did their work by themselves. They were not around their family very much. They also did not see their friends. I like being around people. Cowboys had to know how to take good care of animals. They had to be strong, too. I am too small to take care of big animals. This is not the job for me!

Underline Antonio's topic sentence.

> The topic sentence tells the main idea. It may give an opinion. Here is the correct answer:

I would not have wanted to be a cowboy.

Which of these is a reason that supports Antonio's opinion?

A I enjoy being outdoors.

B Cowboys did their work by themselves.

C Cowboys had to know how to take good care of animals.

D I am too small to take care of big animals.

> Choice A is an opinion. Choices B and C are facts. These are incorrect answers. They do not tell why Antonio does not want to be a cowboy. Choice D tells why Antonio does not like the job of a cowboy. Choice D is the correct answer.

Underline Antonio's closing sentence.

> The closing sentence sums up the ideas of the paragraph. Here is the correct answer:

This is not the job for me!

Test Yourself

Circle the letter of the sentence in each group that would make the best topic sentence of a paragraph.

1   A Some bears are black.

    B Bears come in different colors.

    C Some bears are white.

    D Some bears are brown.

2   A Some ants build homes in trees.

    B Many ants live in nests in the ground.

    C Ants live in many different kinds of homes.

    D Some ants make nests under stones.

3   A Hats help us.

    B Hats keep the sun out of our eyes when we play ball.

    C Rain hats keep the rain off our heads.

    D Hats keep us warm when it is cold.

4 Read the question. Then write a paragraph.

> The passage on pages 33 and 34 is about the job of cowboy. What job would you like to do? Write a paragraph telling about your ideal job. Be sure to:
> - include a topic sentence that tells your main idea
> - use details or reasons to tell why

_____

_____

_____

_____

_____

_____

_____

_____

_____

Main Idea and Details

W.1.2, 5, 6

The **main idea** is what the text is about. The **details** support the text. Or, they explain more about the main idea.

Guided Practice

Read the passage. Then answer the questions.

The Sea Horse

A sea horse is a small fish. It lives in the ocean. It doesn't eat hay. The sea horse eats animals. Some of them are no bigger than the dot on the letter i. These fish are found by the hundreds in seawater.

The sea horse cannot swim fast. It could never catch these quick sea animals. So, the sea horse doesn't even try. Instead, the sea horse hides in the seaweed. These are plants that grow at the bottom of the sea. The sea horse wraps its tail around one and stays out of sight. Soon, the little animals swim by. The sea horse opens a flap on the end of its long nose and pulls in the sea animals. It cannot chew them. The sea horse has no teeth, so it eats its food whole. The sea horse is an interesting fish!

You have learned about sea horses in class. Write a letter to a friend describing the sea horse. This letter should be one paragraph long. Be sure to include:

- a topic sentence that tells your main idea
- details and facts from the passage that support the main idea

Step 1: Prewriting

Read
Note
Organize

Here is how one student, Ariel, answered the question. She used facts and details from the passage. She knew she had to read the question more than once. She underlined important words and made notes.

What key words do you think Ariel underlined?

_____

_____

_____

 Underlining important words helps you know what to write. Remember you want to know the subject and the audience. You also want to know the purpose. Here is a sample answer:

Ariel underlined the words <u>letter</u> and <u>friend</u>. She underlined <u>paragraph</u> and <u>topic sentence</u>. She also underlined <u>main idea</u> and <u>facts and details</u>.

Ariel read the question again. Then she read the passage again. This time she took notes. Here is what she wrote.

Read
Note
Organize

topic: sea horse
I will write for my friend.
A sea horse looks like a horse.
This is how it got its name.
It lives in the sea.
It is a small fish.

First, you should understand the question.
Then you can plan what to write. Ariel decided
to use a web to help her plan. She wrote the main
idea in the center.

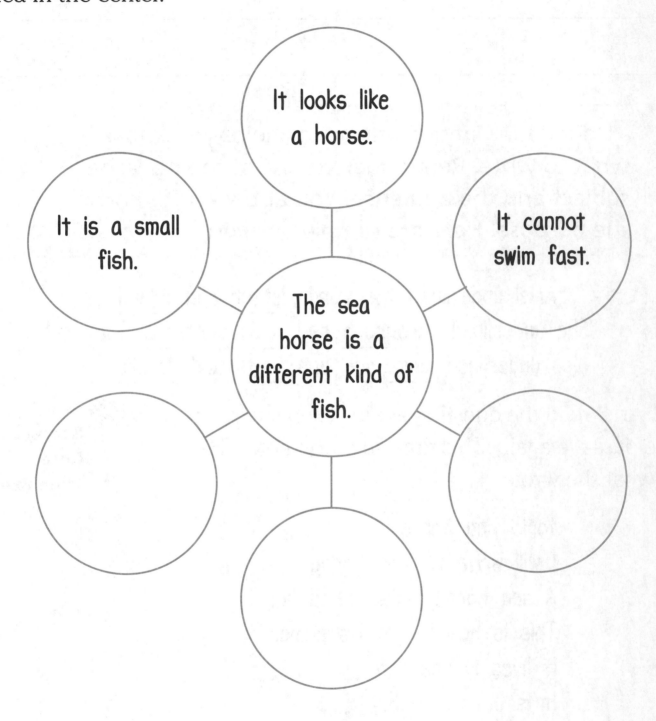

UNIT 1 ▓▓▓▓▓▓▓▓▓▓▓▓▓▓▓▓▓▓▓▓▓▓▓▓▓▓▓▓▓
Elements of Writing

Which details support Ariel's main idea? Put a
check next to the three items that fit into the web.

____ My mom loves sea horses.

____ A sea horse eats little animals.

____ It cannot chew.

____ It hides in seaweed.

The main idea is that sea horses are different
from other fish. The details tell why or how they
are different. Here are the correct answers:

____ My mom loves sea horses.

_✓_ A sea horse eats little animals.

_✓_ It cannot chew.

_✓_ It hides in seaweed.

Ariel is now ready to write her draft.

Step 2: Drafting

Dear Sebastian!

Guess what I learned. I learned about the sea horse. It is a verry different fish. The sea horse looks like a hrose. But it has a curled tail. It lives in the see. The sea horse cannot swim very fast. It hides in the seaweed. Then it swallows little animals that go by. It cannot chew. That is why it is called a sea horse. So it eats its food whole. The sea horse is coool!

Your friend.

Ariel

Which of these sentences is the topic sentence?

    A Guess what I learned.

    B It is a very different fish.

    C It cannot chew.

    D I learned about the sea horse.

The topic sentence tells what the passage is about. It tells the main idea. It is often the first sentence. However, it is not always the first sentence. Choice D is the correct answer. Choices A, B, and C do not tell the main idea.

Why did Ariel tell about the sea horse?

_____

_____

Think about what the question asked. Why is Ariel writing to her friend? Here is a sample answer:

The question said to describe the sea horse.

Step 3: Revising

Read the revised draft carefully. Then answer the questions.

Dear Sebastian!

Guess what I learned. I learned about the sea horse. It is a verry different fish. The sea horse looks like a hrose. But it has a curled tail. It lives *It is a tiny fish.* in the see. The sea horse cannot swim very fast. It hides in the seaweed. Then it swallows little animals that go by. It cannot chew. That is why it is called a sea horse. So it eats its food whole. The sea horse is coool!

Your friend.

Ariel

Why did Ariel move a sentence in the first paragraph?

_____

_____

 Sentences that tell about the same idea should be together. Here is a sample answer:

>   She moved it because it told how the sea horse got its name.

Why did Ariel add a sentence?

_____

_____

 Writers add words or sentences to make their meaning clearer. They also add facts to support the main idea. Here is a sample answer:

>   She added the sentence to tell more about the sea horse.

Peer Review

Ariel might trade papers with a classmate. They would check each other's work. Then they would give it a score based on the checklist. They would discuss ways to improve their work.

Checklist for Writing Main Idea and Details

Score 3

- The writing answers all parts of the question.
- The writing includes a clear main idea.
- The writing includes important details that go with the main idea.
- Words are used correctly and well.
- Capitalization and punctuation are correct.

Score 2

- The writing answers almost all parts of the question.
- The main idea is not completely clear.
- The writing mostly sticks to the topic but there are some details that don't belong.
- Some words are not used correctly.
- There are some mistakes in capitalization and punctuation.

Score 1

- The writing answers only part of the question.
- There is no main idea.
- The writing is missing important details.
- Many words are overused or not used correctly.
- There are many mistakes in capitalization and punctuation.

Step 4: Editing

Read the revised draft on page 46 again. Find and correct six more mistakes.

Mistake 1: _____

Mistake 2: _____

Mistake 3: _____

Mistake 4: _____

Mistake 5: _____

Mistake 6: _____

Look for misspelled words or misplaced punctuation. Did you find all the mistakes? Here are the correct answers:

Mistake 1: Use a comma after the greeting.

Mistake 2: Use a question mark at the end of sentence 1.

Mistake 3: Change hrose to horse in sentence 4.

Mistake 4: Change see to sea in sentence 5.

Mistake 5: Change coool to cool in the last sentence.

Mistake 6: Use a comma after friend in the closing.

Step 5: Publishing

Ariel published her paper by turning it in to her teacher.

Test Yourself

Questions and Answers about Manta Rays

Q What does a manta ray look like?

A The manta ray is shaped like a diamond.
The manta ray also has a long and thin tail.
There are two curved "horns" on its head.
It has an open mouth and black skin. Some
people say it looks like a monster.

Q How does the manta ray swim?

A The manta ray uses its sides. They flap like
wings. But they are really fins.

Q What is its skin like?

A The manta ray has tough skin. It is like
leather.

Q What does a manta ray eat?

A The manta ray eats fish eggs. It also eats
shrimp and small fish. The manta ray eats
plants, too.

Q What family does a manta ray belong to?

A The manta ray belongs to the shark family.
The manta ray is large and very strong like
a shark. However, unlike a shark, the manta
ray is gentle.

You have read about the manta ray. Write
an article for your class newsletter. Tell about
the manta ray. Be sure to include:

• a topic sentence that tells the main idea
• important details about the manta ray

1 What kind of writing are you being asked to do?

Read
Note
Organize

_____

_____

_____

_____

_____

2 Who will read your writing?

_____

_____

_____

_____

_____

UNIT 1 ▨▨▨▨▨▨▨▨▨▨▨▨▨▨▨▨▨▨▨▨▨▨▨▨▨▨ **Read** ▨▨▨
Elements of Writing

3 Fill in the idea web below. This will help you answer the question.

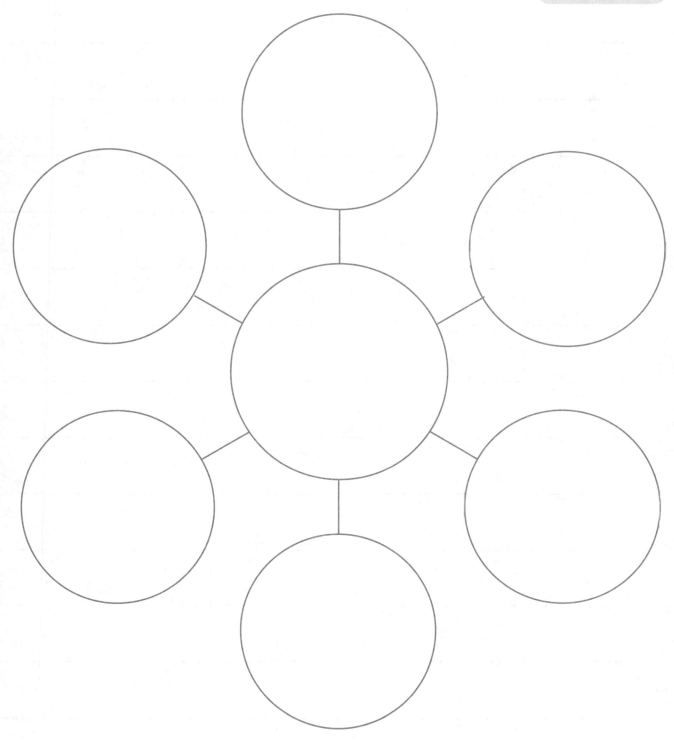

4 Write your draft on the lines below. Look at your web. Think about a topic sentence. Are all your ideas in order? Do you need to add details?

_____

_____

_____

_____

_____

_____

_____

_____

_____

_____

_____

5 Go back over your draft. Make your changes on this page. Check your draft for mistakes. Use the checklist on page 48. Ask a classmate to edit your work if your teacher says to do so.

_____

_____

_____

_____

_____

_____

_____

_____

_____

_____

6 Write your final answer on the lines below. Publish it by showing it to your teacher.

_____

_____

_____

_____

_____

_____

_____

_____

_____

_____

_____

LESSON

4

Cause and Effect

W.1.2, 3, 5, 6

You like to know why something happens. For example, if a book falls from a table, it will make a loud noise. The cause of the sound is the book falling. The loud noise is the effect.

A **cause** is why something happens. An **effect** is what happens. Understanding cause and effect is important. For cause, ask "Why did this happen?" For effect, ask "What happened because of this?"

Your reading makes more sense when you understand these why connections. There are clue words that can help you see cause and effect.

Clue Words for Cause	**Clue Words for Effect**
if	then
because	so
since	this is why
due to	as a result

Where Did the Pie Go?

By Billie Jo Stengel

Father and Ann wanted to surprise Mother. They were going to bake her a blueberry pie. First, they mixed together all the flour and sugar. Then they mixed the other things together. Finally, they baked the pie in the oven. When it was done, Ann took it from the oven. It was very hot. So, she put it on the windowsill to cool. Then she and Father went for a walk.

Soon, Mother came home. Ann was happy to see her. She wanted to show her the surprise. She led Mother into the kitchen. But there was an even bigger surprise. There was no blueberry pie!

Then Ann saw her dog, Spike. He looked strange. His face was purple. And, he was backing away from Ann. He knew that he had done something bad.

At the end of the story, Ann wonders what happened to the pie. Write a note to Ann. Explain what happened to the pie. Be sure to include:

- the reason why the pie is missing
- the word <u>because</u>

Step 1: Prewriting

Read
Note
Organize

Let's look at how one student, Manuel, answered the question. He used details from the story to write an answer to the question. Manuel read the question slowly and carefully.

Then he read it again. This time he underlined important words. These helped him know what to write.

What are some words that Manuel underlined?

_____

_____

Underline words that tell what you are to write. Other important words tell the audience and subject. Here is a sample answer:

<u>note to Ann</u>

Next, Manuel made notes about what to write. Here is what he wrote:

write a note to Ann

tell what happened to the pie

use the word <u>because</u>

Manuel knew he was writing to explain reasons, or causes. He read the passage again to find the details he needed. He used this chart to show the reasons.

Why It Happened (Causes) →	What Happened (Effects)
1. Ann and her father wanted to surprise Mother.	1. Ann and her father made a blueberry pie.
2. The pie was hot.	2. They put the pie on the windowsill.
3. The pie disappeared.	3. Ann was as surprised as Mother.
4. They did not watch the pie.	4. The pie disappeared.
5. Spike ate the pie.	5. Spike had purple on his face.

Step 2: Drafting

Dear Ann.

Do you know what happened to the pie! The pie was on the windowsill. Your Spike dog came into the kitchen. He was hungry. He saw the pie on the windowsill. Then he eight it. Now, he has a purple face. It is because he ate the cherry pie.

Your friend,

Manuel

Find an effect in the letter and underline it.

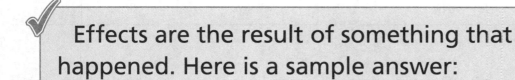

Effects are the result of something that happened. Here is a sample answer:

Now, he has a purple face.

Manuel is now ready to revise his draft.

Step 3: Revising

Dear Ann.

Do you know what happened to the pie! The pie

Then you and your dad went for a walk.

was on the windowsill. ^ Your ~~Spike~~ dog came into

the kitchen. He was hungry. He saw the pie on the

his face is purple.

windowsill. Then he eight it. Now, ~~he has a purple~~

blueberry

~~face.~~ It is because he ate the ^ ~~cherry~~ pie.

Your friend,

Manuel

Why did Manuel add a sentence?

_____

_____

Writers often add details to make their meaning clearer. Here is a sample answer:

Manuel added it to tell why Ann and her father did not see Spike.

Why did Manuel change the order of <u>Spike</u> and <u>dog</u>?

_____

_____

Writers change words to make their meaning clearer. Or, they change words to fix mistakes. Here is a sample answer:

He changed the order because the word <u>dog</u> should come before the dog's name.

Why did Manuel change <u>cherry</u> to <u>blueberry</u>?

_____

_____

Sometimes writers make changes to fix information that is wrong. Here is a sample answer:

The pie was blueberry not cherry.

Peer Review

Manuel used a checklist to check his writing. Then he traded papers with a classmate. They gave each other a score based on the checklist. Then they talked about ways to make their writing better.

Checklist for Writing Cause and Effect

Score 3
- The writing answers all parts of the question.
- The writing has three or more sentences.
- The writing clearly explains the problem and its cause.
- The writing uses the word <u>because</u> correctly.
- The writing stays on the subject.
- Capitalization and punctuation are correct.

Score 2
- The writing answers almost all of the question.
- The writing has two or three sentences.
- The writing explains the problem and its cause.
- The writing uses the word <u>because</u> correctly.
- The writing includes details that are not about the subject.
- There are some mistakes in capitalization and punctuation.

Score 1
- The writing answers only part of the question.
- The writing has two or fewer sentences.
- The writing does not explain the problem or the cause.
- The word <u>because</u> is not used correctly.
- It is hard to tell what the subject is.
- There are many mistakes in capitalization and punctuation.

The next step is for Manuel to edit his work.

Step 4: Editing

Read the revised draft on page 62 again. Find and correct three more mistakes.

Mistake 1: _____

_____

Mistake 2: _____

_____

Mistake 3: _____

✓ This is the last chance to check your work. Look for misspelled words. Look for punctuation that is incorrect. Here are the correct answers:

Mistake 1: Change the period to a comma after the greeting.

Mistake 2: Change the exclamation point to a question mark in sentence 1.

Mistake 3: Change eight to ate in sentence 7.

The last step is for Manuel to publish his work.

Step 5: Publishing

You publish something by sharing it with others. Manuel is ready to share is work. He can do this by turning in his work to the teacher.

Peter and the Dike

A long time ago, there was a boy named Peter. He lived in a town near the sea. The town had dikes built around it. These walls or dams kept the sea from flooding the town. Peter was only 8 years old. But he was strong and brave. His mother and father trusted him to do many things.

One day, Peter's mother baked some nice cakes. "Come," she called to Peter. "Take this basket of cakes to the blind man across the dike."

Peter did as he was asked. Crossing the dike on his way home, he heard something strange. It was the sound of running water. The dike was built to hold the water back. Now, there was a leak in the dike!

Peter jumped down to the bottom of the dike. He reached up and plugged the leak with one finger. Then he called loudly, "Help! Help! A leak in the dike!" Again and again he called. But no answer came. Soon, it became quite dark. Peter feared that he might fall asleep. His hand might slip from the dike. Peter knew very well that he was keeping the sea away from Holland. He knew that people's lives were in his care. No, he could not sleep.

Finally, at first light, a man found Peter. He heard Peter calling. He raced to town to get help. The dike was saved. And the happy people carried Peter home on their shoulders.

The story "Peter and the Dike" tells what happens when Peter takes a basket of cakes to a neighbor. In the middle of the story, Peter has a problem. Write three or more sentences to explain the problem. In your sentences, be sure to

- tell what Peter's problem is
- why he has a problem
- use the word <u>because</u>

1 What kind of writing will you do?

_____

_____

_____

_____

_____

Read
Note
Organize

2 Show how you will plan your sentences. Fill in the chart. Then answer the question.

Read
Note
Organize

Why It Happened (Causes) → What Happened (Effects)

What should you tell about in your first sentence?

_____

_____

_____

UNIT 1 ▒▒
Elements of Writing

3 Write a draft of your sentences. Use your chart and idea about a first sentence. Remember to include the needed details and special word.

_____

_____

_____

_____

_____

_____

_____

_____

_____

_____

_____

4 Read your draft carefully. Rewrite your changes on this page. Edit for mistakes. Use the checklist on page 64 to check your work. Have a classmate review your writing if the teacher says to do so.

_____

_____

_____

_____

_____

_____

_____

_____

_____

_____

5 Write your final copy below. Publish your work by showing it to your teacher.

_____

_____

_____

_____

_____

_____

_____

_____

_____

_____

_____

Alike and Different

W.1.2, 5, 6

Sometimes, you will be asked to tell how two things are alike. This is called **comparing.** You might also be asked how they are different. This is called **contrasting.** There are clue words that tell if two things are alike. There are also key words that tell if two things are different.

Alike Words	**Different Words**
both	unlike
like	but
too	however

Gator or Croc?

Alligators and crocodiles are both reptiles. They have big mouths with sharp teeth. They have strong skin. This skin protects them. They both live in swamps. Both can live as long as 50 years. Both have webbed feet. Both eat only meat. They are carnivores. Alligators live in Florida. Crocodiles do, too.

Gators are smaller than crocs. Crocs can grow to more than 20 feet long. Gators can grow to 15 feet. The alligator has a wide snout. It is shaped like the letter U. You cannot see its teeth when its mouth is closed. The crocodile has a longer snout. It is shaped like a V. Its teeth show even when its mouth is closed. Gators are most active in summer. They feed when the sun sets.

Gators live only in the southern United States and eastern China. However, crocs live in North, South, and Central America. They also live in Africa, Australia, and southeast Asia. Crocs live in saltwater. However, gators live in freshwater.

Write a paragraph or more about alligators and crocodiles. Your audience is your teacher. Show how these reptiles are alike. Then show how they are different. In your answer, be sure to:

- tell how they are alike
- tell how they are different
- use details from the passage

Step 1: Prewriting

This is how one student named Nikki answered the question. She began by reading the question very carefully. She read it until she understood what to write. She underlined important ideas as she read. She underlined

Read
Note
Organize

- the subject
- the kind of writing
- the audience

Which of these is the subject that Nikki underlined?

A paragraph

B teacher

C different

D alligator

Choice D is the correct answer. The subject is the alligator and the crocodile. Choice A is the form the writing should take. Choice B is the audience. Choice C is what you will show in your writing. Choices A, B, and C are incorrect.

Which of these is the type of writing that Nikki is asked to write?

A alike and different

B story

C main idea and details

D cause and effect

Nikki underlines alike and different. This is the type of writing she is being asked to do. Choices B, C, and D are other types of writing. However, these are not what Nikki is being asked to write. They are incorrect.

Nikki read the question. Then she wrote down her ideas. She made a Venn diagram to sort them.

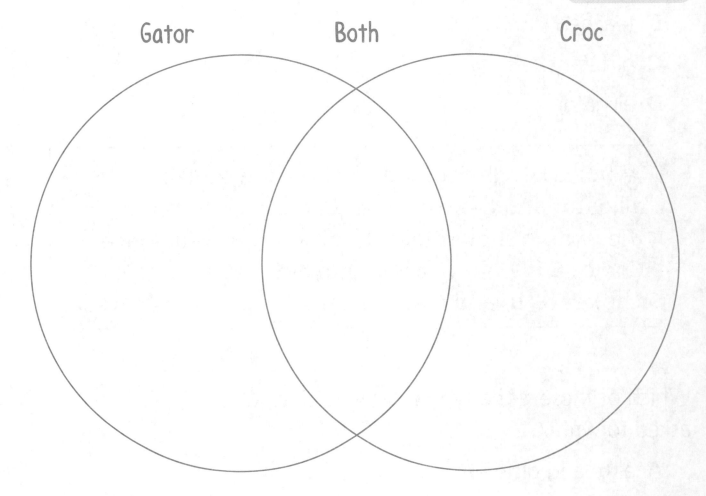

Gator   Both   Croc

Next, Nikki planned her alike and different writing. She wrote her answer in two paragraphs. Her first paragraph tells how they are alike. Her second paragraph tells how they are different.

Look at the Venn diagram. Write the number of the paragraph that matches the detail.

Paragraph 1: Gators and crocs are alike.

Paragraph 2: Gators and crocs are different.

_____ Many people mix up alligators and crocodiles.

_____ Both are reptiles that live in swamps.

_____ Crocs are bigger than gators.

_____ The crocodile has a different snout.

✔ Paragraph 1 should have details that explain how these reptiles are alike. Paragraph 2 will explain how they are different. Here are the correct answers:

__1__ Many people mix up alligators and crocodiles.

__1__ Both are reptiles that live in swamps.

__2__ Crocs are bigger than gators.

__2__ The crocodile has a different snout.

Step 2: Drafting

The croc and gator are alike! Both are reptiles that live in swamps. florida is the place where they both live together. They both eat meat. They have sharp teeth that help them do this. They both like to feed when the sun goes down. They have long snouts. They have webbed feet.

Crocs and gators are different. Crocs are bigger than gators. Their snouts are different. The snout of a gator looks like the letter U. And, you only see its when teeth its mouth is open. The crocodile's snout. looks like the letter V. You can see its teeth when its mouth is closed. The gator and the croc lives in different places. The gator lives in freshwater. It lives in the United States and China. The croc lives in saltwater. It lives in Florida, too. It also lives in other places in the world.

What is the topic sentence in paragraph 1?

A They both eat meat.

B Both are reptiles that live in swamps.

C The croc and gator are alike.

D They have long snouts and webbed feet.

The topic sentence tells the main idea. Choice C is the correct answer. It tells what the paragraph is about. Choices, A, B, and D are incorrect.

What words did Nikki use to compare crocs and gators?

_____

_____

Connecting words give clues. They tell which things are alike. They also tell which things are different. Here is a sample answer:

Nikki used both, too, and also.

The next step is to revise Nikki's draft.

Read the revised draft. Then answer the questions.

Many people think crocs and gators are the same thing, but this is not true.

The croc and gator are alike! Both are reptiles that live in swamps. florida is the _{only} place where they both live together. They both eat meat. They have sharp teeth that help them do this. They both like to feed when the sun goes down. They have long snouts, <del>They have</del> ^{and} webbed feet.

Crocs and gators are different ^{shapes}. Crocs are bigger than gators. Their snouts are different. The snout of a gator looks like the letter U. And, you only see its when teeth its mouth is open. The crocodile's snout. looks like the letter V. You can see its teeth when its mouth is closed. The gator and the croc lives in different places. The gator lives in freshwater. It lives in the United States and China. The croc lives in saltwater. It lives in Florida, too. ^{But} It also lives in other places in the world.

Which sentences did Nikki put together?

_____

_____

 Nikki put two sentences together to describe both reptiles. Here is the correct answer:

They have long snouts. They have webbed feet.

Why did Nikki change the word <u>lives</u> to <u>live</u>?

_____

_____

_____

 Verbs and subjects must agree. More than one thing takes the plain form of a verb. These are things you should look for in this step. Here is a sample answer:

She changed it so the subject and verb would agree.

Peer Review

Nikki used the checklist to check her writing. Then she traded papers with a classmate. They checked each other's writing and gave it a score. They used the checklist to find the score. Then they discussed ways they could each improve their writing.

Checklist for Writing Alike and Different

Score 3
- The writing answers all parts of the question.
- The writing shows two ways the subjects are alike.
- The writing shows two ways the subjects are different.
- The writer uses connecting words.
- There are many good supporting details.
- Capitalization and punctuation are correct.

Score 2
- The writing answers almost all parts of the question.
- The writing shows one way the subjects are alike.
- The writing shows one way the subjects are different.
- The writer uses some connecting words.
- There are some supporting details.
- There are some mistakes in capitalization and punctuation.

Score 1
- The writing answers only part of the question.
- The writing does not show ways the subjects are alike.
- The writing does not show ways the subjects are different.
- The writer uses few or no connecting words.
- There are not many supporting details.
- There are many mistakes in capitalization and punctuation.

Now, Nikki is ready to edit her work.

Step 4: Editing

Read the revised draft again on page 80. Find and correct two more mistakes.

Mistake 1: _____

Mistake 2: _____

Mistake 3: _____

In this step, you look for misspelled words. You also look for the wrong punctuation. Here are the correct answers:

Mistake 1: Change the exclamation point to a period in sentence 2.

Mistake 2: Capitalize Florida in sentence 4.

Mistake 3: Take out period after snout in sentence 14.

Step 5: Publishing

Nikki published her paper by turning in her work to her teacher.

Twins

Everyone asks how I can tell my twin sisters apart. It's easy. I can tell by looking at them. Both have straight brown hair. But Beth has a peak at the back of her head. Her hair sweeps back more. They both have gray-green eyes. But Barb's right eye is little bigger than her left. Beth has three freckles under her left eye. Barb doesn't. They are both four feet, six inches tall. But Barb moves in a calm way. She seems taller. Beth is a quicker. Beth is left-handed. Barb is right-handed.

Write two paragraphs about the twins. One paragraph should tell how they are alike. One paragraph should tell how they are different. Be sure to:

- tell at least two ways that they are alike
- tell at least two ways that they are different
- use details from the paragraph to support your answer

1 What kind of writing are you being asked to do?

_____

_____

_____

_____

2 What form will your writing take?
(Hint: two sentences, two paragraphs, or one paragraph)

_____

_____

_____

_____

UNIT 1 ░░░░░░░░░░░░░░░░░░░░░░░░░░░░░░░░░░ Read ░░░
Elements of Writing

3 Fill in the circles in the Venn diagram. Use details from your reading. This will help you see what is the same and what is different.

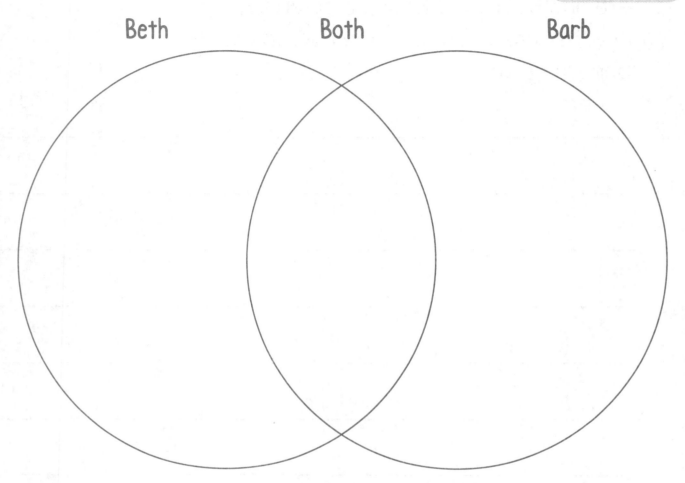

Beth   Both   Barb

What will you put in each paragraph? List ideas from your Venn diagram.

Paragraph 1: _____

_____

Paragraph 2: _____

_____

4 Write your draft. Use your plan to help you write. Be sure you start each paragraph with a topic sentence. In paragraph 1, tell how Barb and Beth are alike. In paragraph 2, tell how they are different. Remember to use connecting words.

_____

_____

_____

_____

_____

_____

_____

_____

_____

_____

UNIT 1 ▓▓▓▓▓▓▓▓▓▓▓▓▓▓▓▓▓▓▓▓▓▓▓▓▓▓▓▓▓▓▓▓▓▓▓▓
Elements of Writing

5 Read back over your draft. Make your changes on this page. Check your draft for mistakes. Use the checklist on page 83 to review your own writing. Ask a classmate to edit your work if your teacher tells you to do so.

_____

_____

_____

_____

_____

_____

_____

_____

_____

_____

6 Write your final answer below. Publish it by showing it to your teacher.

_____

_____

_____

_____

_____

_____

_____

_____

_____

_____

_____

_____

Types of Writing

You use the same writing steps every time you write. But the kinds of writing you do are different. You might write a story. Or, you might write to tell about something. Writing a story is different than writing for information. This unit will tell about the different kinds of writing.

- **In Lesson 6,** you will write about what you think. This is an opinion. You will use facts in your writing. These facts will help support your opinion.

- **Lesson 7** is about descriptive writing. In this kind of writing, you tell what something looks like. You create a word picture of the scene for your readers.

- **In Lesson 8,** you'll write a narrative. A narrative is a story with a beginning, middle, and end. A story also has a setting. It has characters, too.

- **Lesson 9** tells how to write for information. This is the writing you do in class and on tests.

Reasoned Writing

W.1.1, 5, 6

Sometimes, you write to persuade. That means you want someone to think the way you do.

Your writing should have a topic sentence. This sentence should tell what you want your reader to believe or do. You will be giving your opinion. An **opinion** is what you believe or think. After that, you want to write the facts, examples, and reasons that back up your opinion. A **fact** is a true statement. It can be proved. Your last sentence should sum up your paragraph with a strong ending.

Guided Practice

Read the question below. Then write a response.

You want to write a short book report to persuade your classmates to read your favorite book. Be sure to:

- give your opinion clearly in the first sentence
- use facts and examples in your supporting sentences

Step 1: Prewriting

Here is how one student, DeShawn, looked at the question. He read the question carefully. Some words were clues. The words <u>to persuade</u> and <u>give your opinion</u> told DeShawn that he was being asked to write a persuasive paragraph.

Read
Note
Organize

DeShawn read the question one more time. He knows he would need to convince someone else to read the book. He had to make sure his facts were strong.

Read
Note
Organize

The next step is to make a plan of what you will write. Your plan can help you make your thoughts clear. You need to make a plan that works well for the kind of writing you will do.

Read
Note
Organize

This question asks DeShawn to write a short book report for his classmates. The report has to give an opinion in the first sentence. It has to use facts and examples in supporting sentences. DeShawn chose to use a simple main opinion and facts chart. This chart will help him put together the facts for his paragraph.

Main Opinion:

| |
| |

↕

Facts:

| 1. |
| |

| 2. |
| |

| 3. |
| |

| 4. |
| |

Read DeShawn's draft. Then answer the questions

My favorite book:

Harold and the Purple Crayon

The best book in the world is Harold and the purple Crayon. Crockett Johnson. wrote it. My dad bought it for me when I was 2 years old. I could read it. So, dad read it to me.

The book is about a little boy named Harold. Harold is curious. He loves to draw. He uses a crayon purple to draw the places he wants to go. This letss him explore the world. He wants to go to the moon. But there is no moon that night. So, Harold draws a moon. There is no way to get there. So, he uses the crayon to draw a path to the moon. He visits other places, too. Then he uses the crayon to come home again.

I think this book is grate. First, the author seems to say if we can dream it, then we can do it. There is always a way We just need to figure it out. Second, it tells us that there is no place like home. Harold goes many places. But he always comes home. Third, this book shows how fun drawing can be. It let you create new worlds.

Underline DeShawn's topic sentence.

 The topic sentence should state the main idea. Here is a sample answer:

The best book in the world is <u>Harold and the Purple Crayon</u>.

Does his last sentence work well? Why or why not?

_____

_____

 The last sentence should sum up the main points. This is the closing sentence. Here is a sample answer:

No, he does not have a closing sentence.

Read DeShawn's revised draft. Then answer the questions.

My favorite book:

<u>Harold and the Purple Crayon</u>

The best book in the world is <u>Harold and the</u>

<u>purple Crayon</u>. Crockett Johnson̸ wrote it.

My dad bought it for me when I was 2 years old.

I could _{not}̂ read it. So, dad read it to me.

The book is about a little boy named Harold.

Harold is curious. He loves to draw. He uses a

⬚crayon⬚ ⬚purple⬚ to draw the places he wants to

go. This lets̸ him explore the world. He wants to go

to the moon. But there is no moon that night. So,

Harold draws a moon. There is no way to get

there. So, he uses the crayon to draw a path to

the moon. He visits other places, too. Then he

uses the crayon to come home again.

I think this book is grate. First, the author

seems to say if we can dream it, then we can do

it. There is always a way We just need to figure

it out. Second, it tells us that there is no place

like home. Harold goes many places. But he always

comes home. Third, this book shows how much fun

drawing can be. It let s you create new worlds. Everyone

should read Harold and the Purple Crayon!

What word did DeShawn add to sentence 4?

A purple

B crayon

C not

D come

Choice C is the correct answer. DeShawn added the word <u>not</u> in sentence 4. Choices A, B, and D are incorrect. These were words that had changes. But they were already in the story.

UNIT 2 ▒▒▒
Types of Writing

Why did he add it?

_____

_____

 Writers often add words to make their meaning clearer. Here is a sample answer:

He added the word to give the correct meaning. He did not know how to read.

Peer Review

The next step is to make sure the writing fits the checklist. DeShawn used the checklist to review his writing. Then he traded papers with another student. They reviewed each other's writing and gave it a score based on the checklist. Then they discussed ways they could improve their writing.

Checklist for Writing to Persuade

Score 3
- The writing answers all parts of the question.
- The opening sentence states the writer's opinion.
- The details use facts, not opinions, to convince readers.
- Words are used correctly and well.
- Capitalization and punctuation are correct.

Score 2
- The writing answers almost all parts of the question.
- The opening sentence doesn't state the writer's opinion very clearly.
- Some of the details use facts to convince readers.
- Some words are misused.
- There are some mistakes in capitalization and punctuation.

Score 1
- The writing answers only part of the question.
- The opening sentence states a fact.
- The details do not use facts to convince readers.
- Many words are overused or misused.
- There are many mistakes in capitalization and punctuation.

DeShawn is now ready to edit his paper.

Step 4: Editing

Proofread DeShawn's revised draft on pages 97 – 98 for three more mistakes. Write your corrections on the draft.

Find and correct 3 mistakes in DeShawn's draft.

Mistake 1: _____

Mistake 2: _____

_____

Mistake 3: _____

Read over the revised draft. Do you see any misspelled words? Look for missing periods and other punctuation. Check that words are capitalized correctly. Here are the correct answers:

Mistake 1: Capitalize the d in dad in sentence 5.

Mistake 2: Change the word grate to great in the first sentence in paragraph 3.

Mistake 3: Add a period after way in sentence 20.

Step 5: Publishing

The last step is to share what you have written. There are many ways to publish something. You can turn in your work to your teacher. You can read it aloud to your classmates. Or, you can put it in the class newsletter.

Read the passage. Then answer the questions.

Birthday Celebrations

We all have a birthday. But we don't celebrate it the same way. In the United States, people have a special cake with candles on top. They must blow out the candles in one breath. In China, they eat special noodles for lunch. They are a wish for a long life. In Korea, people have seaweed soup. They also eat rice cakes. These cakes have nuts and fruits. In Russia, they have a birthday pie. It has a message carved into the crust. In India, children share chocolates with classmates. There are many ways to celebrate a birthday!

Write an article for the class newsletter. Tell what you think is the best way to celebrate a birthday. Be sure to:

- give your opinion clearly in the first sentence
- use facts and examples in your supporting sentences

1 What kind of writing are you being asked to do?

Read
Note
Organize

_____

_____

_____

_____

_____

2 Who will read your writing?

_____

_____

_____

_____

_____

3 Fill in the opinion and reason chart below. This will help you answer the question.

Main Opinion:

Reasons:

1.

2.

3.

4.

UNIT 2 ▚▚
Types of Writing

4 Use your chart to help you write your draft. Be sure to tell your opinion. Then write each reason for your opinion.

_____

_____

_____

_____

_____

_____

_____

_____

_____

_____

_____

_____

5 Now, check your draft for any mistakes. Make your changes on this page. Use the checklist on page 100 to review your writing. Have a classmate edit your writing if your teacher allows it.

_____

_____

_____

_____

_____

_____

_____

_____

_____

_____

6 Write your final copy on this page. Publish it by
showing it to your teacher.

_____

_____

_____

_____

_____

_____

_____

_____

_____

_____

Descriptive Writing

W.1.2, 5, 6, 8

Sometimes, you want to tell about something. You tell what an apple looks like. Or, you tell what a car sounds like. You write to **describe.** You use words to paint a picture. You paint a word picture by telling what you see, hear, smell, taste, and feel.

Guided Practice

Read the question. Then write a response.

Your teacher has given your class a project. You have been asked to write a paragraph about a part of your neighborhood or town that you like to explore. Use details to tell about the place. Be sure to:

- tell what it looks like
- tell what it feels like
- tell what it sounds like
- tell what it smells like

Step 1: Prewriting

Now you will see how one student, Fisher, thought about the question. First, he read the question carefully. He made sure he understood what the question was asking.

Read
Note
Organize

Then he underlined key words. This helped him know what to write.

Read
Note
Organize

Which key words did Fisher underline?

_____

_____

_____

Fisher needs to know the subject he is writing about. He also needs to know the form. No audience is given. He knows he is writing for his teacher. Here is a sample answer:

Fisher underlined <u>write a paragraph</u>. He also underlined <u>tell about the place</u>. He underlined <u>looks like</u>, <u>feels like</u>, <u>sounds like</u>, and <u>smells like</u>.

The next step is to plan what you will write. Charts and webs can help you put your ideas in order. This question asked Fisher to describe a place. He needed to use details about how the place looks, sounds, smells, and feels. Fisher chose a senses chart to help him.

Read
Note
Organize

Subject: Children's Castle
Sights
lots of children, rope net, sings, trees, wooden castle, children running, swinging on swing
Sounds
children laughing and talking
Smells
suntan lotion
Tastes
cool water
Touch
warm from sun and running, rough wood, breeze, scratchy rope
Thoughts/Feelings
this is so cool I do not want to go home

Read each detail. Each detail goes with a sense. Label each item with the correct sense. Use the word **sight, sound, smell, touch,** or **feelings.**

_____ The children are calling each other's names.

_____ A little girl is crying because she does not want to leave.

_____ The slide is warm when I sit on it.

_____ I can smell the sunscreen my mom put on me.

_____ I see children climbing the steps to the castle walkway above.

> ✓ **Each sentence gives a clue about the sense that is used. The sentence may name the sense. Or, it may give details that help you know the sense that was used. Here are the correct answers:**

__sound__ The children are calling each other's names.

__feelings__ A little girl is crying because she does not want to leave.

__touch__ The slide is warm when I sit on it.

__smell__ I can smell the sunscreen my mom put on me.

__sight__ I see children climbing the steps to the castle walkway above.

I go to the Children's Castle with my mom every Saturday. It is a playground inside a castle. It is not a castle real. It is built of wood to look like one. We get out of the car and walk up to the gate. We can only see the walls and towers. But we hear children laughing. When we come through the gate, I can see children playing on the swings and slide. First, I climb the stairs in one of the towers? I walk on on the walkway above the playground. I grab the scratchy rope and use the rope net to climb down to the ground. I can smell the sunscreen my mom put on me. A breeze blows my hair in my eyes. Then I see my friends. I call their names and run to them. We play on monkey bars. Then play hide and seek. "Fisher," my mom says. I know what is coming. I don't want to leave because I am having too much fun. This is such a cool place that I never want to go home.

What sentence tells what Fisher is describing?

_____

_____

> ✓ A paragraph needs to have a topic sentence. This tells what the paragraph is about. Here is a sample answer:

I go to the Children's Castle with my mom every Saturday.

List two details that Fisher gives about the Children's Castle.

_____

_____

> ✓ The details help you picture the place. The writer tells what the place looks like and what it sounds like. Here is a sample answer:

I walk on the walkway above the playground.
I see children playing on the swings and slide.

Fisher is now ready to revise what he has written.

Step 3: Revising

I go to the Children's Castle with my mom every Saturday. It is a playground inside a castle. It is not a castle real. It is built of wood to look like one. We get out of the car and walk up to the gate. We can only see the walls and towers. But we hear children laughing. When we come through the gate, I ~~can~~ see children playing on the swings and slide. First, I climb the stairs in one of the towers? I walk on on the walkway above the playground. I grab the scratchy rope and use the rope net to climb down to the ground. I can smell the sunscreen my mom put on me. A breeze blows my hair in my eyes. Then I see my friends. I call their names and run to them. We play on monkey bars. Then we play hide and seek. "Fisher," my mom says. I know what is coming. I don't want to leave because I am having too much fun. This is such a cool place that I never want to go home.

Why did Fisher add the word <u>we</u>?

_____

_____

A complete sentence has a subject and a verb.
The reader should know who is doing something.
The subject tells this. Here is a sample answer:

The sentence did not have a subject.

Why did Fisher switch the order of two words?

_____

_____

Writers need to make sure that their meaning is
clear. Here is a sample answer:

The sentence does not make sense.

Peer Review

Fisher used the checklist to check his writing.
Then he traded papers with a classmate. They
checked each other's writing. Then they gave it a
score based on the checklist. They talked about
ways they could improve their writing.

Checklist for Writing to Describe

Score 3
- The writing answers all parts of the question.
- The details use words related to the five senses.
- The last sentence gives a clear feeling about the subject.
- Words are used correctly and well.
- Capitalization and punctuation are correct.

Score 2
- The writing answers almost all parts of the question.
- Some of the details use words related to the five senses.
- The last sentence gives some feeling about the subject.
- Some words are misused.
- There are some mistakes in capitalization and punctuation.

Score 1
- The writing answers only part of the question.
- The details don't use words related to the five senses.
- The last sentence does not give a clear feeling about the subject.
- Many words are overused or misused.
- There are many mistakes in capitalization and punctuation.

Fisher is now ready to edit his paper.

Step 4: Editing

Reread Fisher's revised draft on page 114. Then find and correct three mistakes.

Mistake 1: _____

_____

Mistake 2: _____

_____

Mistake 3: _____

Check for any words that are not spelled correctly. Look for missing punctuation. Or, look for punctuation that is not right. Here are the correct answers:

Mistake 1: Change the question mark to a period in sentence 9.

Mistake 2: Delete the second word on in sentence 10.

Mistake 3: Add the before monkey in sentence 16.

Step 5: Publishing

Fisher is ready to share his work. He can use a computer to type his work. Then he can turn in his work to the teacher.

Mix A Pancake

By Christina Rossetti

Mix a pancake,
    Stir a pancake,
        Pop it in the pan;
Fry the pancake,
Toss the pancake,—
    Catch it if you can.

Write a paragraph describing the kitchen where you make pancakes. Use details to help you write. Be sure to:

- describe the details using words about the five senses (sight, sound, smell, taste, and touch)

- write a topic sentence that tells the subject

- write a last sentence that tells how you feel about the subject

1 What kind of writing are you being asked to do? How do you know?

_____

_____

_____

_____

2 What are you being asked to write about?

_____

_____

_____

_____

_____

3 Use this chart to help plan your answer.

Subject: Making Pancakes in My Kitchen
Sights
Sounds
Smells
Tastes
Touch
Thoughts/Feelings

4 Write your draft. Look at your chart. Think about how your topic sentence talks about the subject. Think about details that tell about the subject.

_____

_____

_____

_____

_____

_____

_____

_____

_____

_____

_____

5 Look over your draft. Make your changes on this page. Edit your draft. Use the checklist on page 116 to review the paper. Ask a classmate to review it if the teacher tells you to do so.

_____

_____

_____

_____

_____

_____

_____

_____

_____

_____

UNIT 2
Types of Writing

6 Write your final answer on this page. Then publish your work by showing it to your teacher.

_____

_____

_____

_____

_____

_____

_____

_____

_____

_____

_____

_____

Narrative Writing

W.1.3, 5, 6, 8

When you tell a story, you need a clear beginning, middle, and end. You need **characters,** too. These are the people in the story. You need to tell where the story took place. You need to tell when it took place. This is the **setting.**

Guided Practice

Read the question. Then answer the questions.

Write a story for your classmates about a time you made a new friend. Be sure to:

- write details in the order they happened
- write a paragraph

Step 1: Prewriting

Here is how one student, Karlee, answered the question. She read the question carefully. The words <u>write a story</u> told her what she needed to write. The story was about a <u>time you made a new friend</u>.

Read
Note
Organize

Karlee read the question again. She looked for key words about how to tell the story. The words <u>in the order they happened</u> let her know she should use time order.

Read
Note
Organize

The next step is to plan what you will write. A chart can help you write down your ideas. Karlee chose this chart to help her sort her ideas.

Read
Note
Organize

Subject: A Time I Made a New Friend	
1	I just moved to my new house.
2	I looked out the window.
3	I saw boys and girls playing outside.
4	
5	
6	

What do you think happened next? Number the sentences 4, 5, and 6 in the order they took place.

_____ A girl knocked at the door and asked me to come play with them.

_____ I made a new friend.

_____ I went to watch TV.

> ✓ Sometimes, one thing causes another. Think about what happened. Then think about why it happened. This will help you know the order of events. Here is the correct answer:

__5__ A girl knocked at the door and asked me to come play with them.

__6__ I made a new friend.

__4__ I went to watch TV.

Read Karlee's draft. Then answer the questions.

I had just moved to our new house. I was sad because I had no friends I did not know anyone. On the day second, I looked out the window of my new house. Boys and girls were running. They were laughing and jumping. I wanted to play, too. But I did not know any of them. I really missed my old house and friends.

I went to turn on the TV. Soon, I heard someone at the door. A girl said, "My name is rachel. I saw you looking out the window. Would you like to play?" "I sure would!" I said. She smiled.

We played all afternoon. I learned many new games. And I made a new friend. We've been best friends ever since!

What is the main idea of the story?

_____

_____

✓ The main idea is often told in the topic sentence. Here is a sample answer:

I was sad because I had moved and had no friends.

What words help you know the order of events?

_____

_____

✓ Some words give clues about what happened first or last. Here is the correct answer:

second day, Soon

Step 3: Revising

I had just moved to ~~our~~ ^my^ new house. I was sad because I had no friends I did not know anyone. On the [day] second, I looked out the window of my new house. Boys and girls were running. They were laughing and jumping. I wanted to play, too. But I did not know any of them. I really missed my old house and friends.

I went to turn on the TV. Soon, I heard someone ^knocking^ at the door. A girl said, "My name is rachel. I saw you looking out the window. Would you like to play?" "I sure would!" I said. She smiled.

We played all afternoon. I learned many new games. And I made a new friend. We've been best friends ever since!

Why did Karlee change the order of the words?

_____

_____

 Writers change words to make their meaning clearer. Here is a sample answer:

Karlee changed the order because the sentence did not make sense.

Peer Review

The next step is to have a classmate check your writing. Karlee used a checklist to check her writing. Then she traded papers with a classmate. They reviewed each other's writing and gave it a score based on the checklist. Then they talked about ways they could improve their writing.

Checklist for Writing a Story

Score 3
- The writing answers all parts of the question.
- There is a clear beginning, middle, and end to the story.
- Details are interesting and are in a sensible order.
- The place and time of the story are clear.
- Capitalization and punctuation are correct.

Score 2
- The writing answers almost all parts of the question.
- Parts of the beginning, middle, or end to the story are not clear.
- Not all details are in order or make sense.
- The place and time of the story are not clear.
- There are some mistakes in capitalization and punctuation.

Score 1
- The writing answers only part of the question.
- There is not a clear beginning, middle, or end to the story.
- Many details are missing or the order is unclear.
- The writer doesn't describe the place or time of the story.
- There are many mistakes in capitalization and punctuation

Karlee is now ready to edit her paper.

Step 4: Editing

Find and correct two mistakes in Karlee's draft.

Mistake 1: _____

Mistake 2: _____

Check for any mistakes in punctuation. Are the words spelled right? Here are the correct answers:

Mistake 1: <u>Add a period after friends in sentence 2.</u>

Mistake 2: <u>Capitalize the name rachel in sentence 11.</u>

The last step is for Karlee to publish her work.

Step 5: Publishing

There are many ways to share a story. Karlee can use a computer to write her story. Then she can give a copy to her teacher. She can read the story to her classmates or family. She could even enter it into a writing contest.

The Wagon

One spring afternoon, Sandy got her wagon out of the shed. It had been in there all winter.

"My wagon looks old!" Sandy said. It no longer looked shiny and new.

Sandy's mother looked at the wagon. "We need to buy some paint," she said.

Sandy and her mother walked to the store. They bought a can of red paint. Then they went home. Sandy found the paintbrushes. Then her mother showed her how to paint the wagon. Sandy began painting the wagon. Soon, she stood back and looked at it.

"Now, my wagon looks new!" said Sandy.

Do you remember a time that you solved a problem? You may have fixed it on your own. Maybe you had help. Write a story about a time you solved a problem. Be sure to:

- write events in the order that they happened

- use details to make the story seem real

- write about the place and time of the story

1 What kind of writing are you being asked to do?

Read
Note
Organize

_____

_____

_____

_____

_____

2 Use the chart to write down your ideas. Make sure they are in the order in which they happened.

Read
Note
Organize

Subject: A Time I Fixed a Problem	
1	
2	
3	
4	
5	
6	

3 Write your draft. First, look at your chart. Think about the main subject of the paragraph. Make sure the events are in time order.

_____

_____

_____

_____

_____

_____

_____

_____

_____

_____

UNIT 2
Types of Writing

4 Check your work. Make any changes on this page. Edit your draft for any mistakes. Use the checklist on page 131 to check your paper. Have a classmate check your writing if your teacher lets you do so.

_____

_____

_____

_____

_____

_____

_____

_____

_____

_____

5 Write your final copy on the lines below. Publish
your work by showing it to your teacher.

_____

_____

_____

_____

_____

_____

_____

_____

_____

_____

_____

Informational Writing

W.1.2, 5, 6, 8

When you write a report, you tell facts or you explain something. You write to give **information.** You also may do this kind of writing when you answer a question.

You can set up your writing in a few ways. One way is by main idea and details. Another way is to write steps in the right order.

Guided Practice

Read the question. Then write a response.

Write a paragraph that tells how you created something. You will share your paragraph with your classmates. Use words that tell the order of the steps. Be sure to:

- put the steps in order
- write all the steps you follow

Step 1: Prewriting

Read
Note
Organize

Here is how one student, Jasmine, answered the question. She read the question carefully. Then she underlined key words.

What words did Jasmine underline?

_____

_____

_____

The writer needs to know what she will write. She needs to know how long it will be. Will it be one paragraph? Will it be longer? She needs to know who will read it. Here is a sample answer:

Jasmine underlined <u>steps in order</u>. She underlined <u>paragraph</u>. She also underlined <u>how you created something</u>. Jasmine underlined <u>classmates</u>.

UNIT 2
Types of Writing

140

© The Continental Press, Inc. DUPLICATING THIS MATERIAL IS ILLEGAL.

The next step is to plan your writing. A plan helps you sort your ideas. Then you can make sure they are in the right order. Jasmine used a sequence chart to help her put the steps in the right order.

How to Make Play Dough
Step 1   Mix flour with salt in a bowl.
Step 2   Mix oil with water.
Step 3
Step 4
Step 5

Read the steps below. Which ones complete the chart on page 141? Label your choices 3, 4, and 5 in that order.

_____ Pour the water and oil into the flour mixture.

_____ Mash it all together with your hands.

_____ Add food coloring to the oil and water.

> **Think about what you do first, second, and so on. Sometimes, you must do something before you can do something else. It is important to list tasks in order. Here is a sample answer:**

__4__ Pour the water and oil into the flour mixture.

__5__ Mash it all together with your hands.

__3__ Add food coloring to the oil and water.

Jasmine has planned her writing. Now, she is ready to start writing.

Step 2: Drafting

Making Your Own Play Dough

Play dough is fun to play with. You can buy it at a store, or your can make your own. here is one way to do it.

First, mix two cups of flour with one cap of salt in a bowl. Then, in a cup, mix two spoonfuls of oil with one cup of water. Next, add four drops of food coloring to the cup of oil and water.

Slowly, pour the wet stuff in the cup into the mixing bowl Mash it all together with your hands. When it is mixed, you have play dough.

What words does Jasmine use to show the order
of the steps?

_____

_____

 Connecting words help the reader understand the order of events. These words can be <u>first</u>, <u>second</u>, and <u>last</u>. Or, they might be words like <u>before</u>, <u>after</u>, or <u>then</u>. Here is a sample answer:

She uses <u>First</u>, <u>Then</u>, and <u>Next</u>.

Jasmine's next step is to revise her writing.

Step 3: Revising

Making Your Own Play Dough

Play dough is fun to play with. You can buy it

at a store, or your can make your own. here is

This will make one color of play dough.

one way to do it.

First, mix two cups of flour with one cap of

salt in a bowl. Then, in a cup, mix two spoonfuls

of oil with one cup of water. Next, add four drops

of food coloring to the cup of oil and water.

Slowly, pour the wet stuff in the cup into the

mixing bowl Mash it all together with your hands.

When it is mixed, you have play dough.

Why did Jasmine add a sentence?

_____

_____

 Revising means fixing any problems with your writing. This might mean rewriting long sentences. Or, it might mean adding words or sentences. Here is a sample answer:

She wanted to make it clear that the steps only made one color of dough.

Peer Review

Jasmine used a checklist to check that her writing was complete. Then she traded papers with a classmate. They looked at each other's work. Then they gave it a score based on the checklist. They discussed ways they could improve their writing.

Checklist for Writing to Give Information

Score 3

- The writing answers all parts of the question.
- The topic sentence tells a main idea.
- Details support the main idea.
- The writing uses many connecting words.
- Capitalization and punctuation are correct.

Score 2

- The writing answers almost all parts of the question.
- There is a main idea.
- Some details support the main idea.
- The writing uses some connecting words.
- There are some mistakes in capitalization and punctuation.

Score 1

- The writing answers only part of the question.
- The main idea is unclear.
- Few details support the main idea.
- The writing does not use connecting words.
- There are many mistakes in capitalization and punctuation.

Now, Jasmine can edit her paper.

Step 4: Editing

Reread Jasmine's revised draft on page 145. Find and correct three more mistakes.

Mistake 1: _____

Mistake 2: _____

Mistake 3: _____

_____

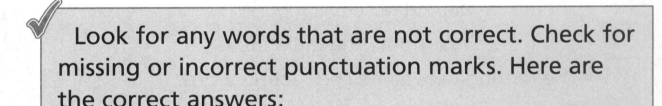

Look for any words that are not correct. Check for missing or incorrect punctuation marks. Here are the correct answers:

Mistake 1: Change your to you in sentence 2.
Mistake 2: Change cap to cup in sentence 4.
Mistake 3: Add a period after the word bowl in sentence 7.

Step 5: Publishing

The last step is to share your writing. Jasmine can use a computer to type her informational writing. Then she can turn in her work to her teacher. She could also use her work to make a poster telling the steps.

Maps

Maps can help us learn about the world around us. A map is a drawing. It shows part of the earth. Maps use lines, words, and colors. Everything on a map is smaller than in real life.

There are many kinds of maps. Each kind of map helps people in a different way. You might use a map to get from home to school. Families need road maps for trips. Maps help airplanes fly. They can also tell us about weather. We can learn how much rain falls in an area from maps.

Many people work together to make a map. First, map makers walk around. They write down what they see. These notes help them draw the new map. Then they might take pictures from an airplane. Finally, everything is put together.

The new map might show streets. It might show schools, libraries, and other buildings.

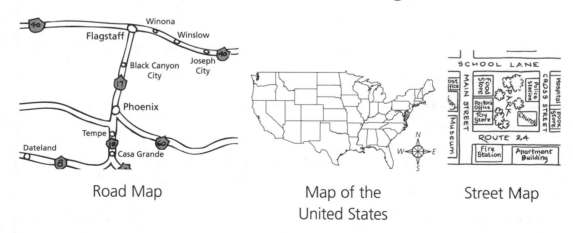

Road Map   Map of the United States   Street Map

Write a paragraph for your teacher about maps and how they are made. Tell what you know. Use details from the article and art. Be sure to:

- have a topic sentence
- use connecting words like <u>first</u>, <u>second</u>, <u>then</u>, or <u>now</u>

1 What kind of writing are you being asked to do?

Read
Note
Organize

_____

_____

_____

_____

_____

2 Who will read your writing?

_____

_____

_____

_____

3 Use the chart to help you plan your writing. What was the sequence of events?

Main idea:
What maps are used for
How maps are made

4 Write your draft below. Use your chart to help you write your draft. Think about the topic sentence. Use connecting words.

_____

_____

_____

_____

_____

_____

_____

_____

_____

_____

_____

5 When you have finished your draft, look over your work. Make your changes on this page. Edit your draft. Use the checklist on page 147 to review your work. Have a classmate edit it if your teacher says to do so.

_____

_____

_____

_____

_____

_____

_____

_____

_____

_____

6 Write your final copy on this page. Publish your work by showing it to your teacher.

_____

_____

_____

_____

_____

_____

_____

_____

_____

_____

_____

_____

Research

You know how to write for a test. You also know how to write for the classroom. This unit looks at a different kind of writing. The research paper is a report. You will learn how to find facts. Then you will learn how to organize it.

- **Lesson 10** tells how to find a topic. It also tells how to find facts.

- **In Lesson 11,** you'll learn how to write a strong thesis statement. You'll also learn how to sort your facts. An outline will help you do this.

- **Lesson 12** is about how to write a research paper. This lesson will help you create a source list. It will also help you pick visual aids for your paper.

Researching Sources and Content

W.1.2, 5–8

Often, we are asked to share what we know. Writing a report is one way to do this. You find out about something. Then you write about what you learned.

This kind of writing is done in steps. These are the steps.

Step 1: Pick a topic.
This is the subject.

Step 2: Research the topic.
This is how we find out more about something.

Step 3: Develop the thesis statement.
This is the main idea.

Step 4: Outline the paper.
This is the plan to help write the paper.

Step 5: Write the paper.
This is putting ideas and facts together.

Step 6: Tell the sources.
This is telling where we found our facts.

Step 1: Pick a Topic

    The first step is to know what you will write about. Your teacher may tell you what to write about. Or, you may be asked to pick what to write about. The topic should be just right. It should be something you can write about in a few paragraphs or pages. This means you need to make sure that your topic is not too big.

Guided Practice

Read the question. Then answer it.

Which of these would take a few paragraphs to write about?

    A mammals

    B the cat family

    C lions and tigers

    D the house cat

    Did you pick D? Choice D is a topic that can be covered in a few paragraphs. Choices A, B, and C are about more than one animal. There are too many animals to write about. You might need to write a paragraph about each animal.

Step 2: Research the Topic

Now, you will find facts about your topic. Your teacher may give you questions to answer about the topic. Or, you may need to ask your own questions. Think about what you know about the topic. Then think about important questions that you would like to answer.

Your teacher may tell you where to look for facts. Or, you may need to find the facts yourself. There are many ways to find facts. You can

- ask someone who knows about the topic
- read a book about it
- check a website
- look in a reference book

There are parts in a book that can help you with your fact finding. The **table of contents** is at the front of a book. It tells the names of the chapters in the book. It tells what page they start on.

All Kinds of Games
Table of Contents

Chapter 1	History of Games	5
Chapter 2	Board Games	10
Chapter 3	Sports	25
Chapter 4	Playground Games	40
Index		50

You can read the names of the chapters. They may have words that relate to your subject. Then you can check the chapter to see if there are facts you can use.

As you read the chapter, look at the **headings.** They break the text into smaller sections. They may have words related to your subject. Headings are usually in bold print.

Also, check the **index** at the back of the book. It lists subjects in ABC order. It shows page numbers. Readers turn to these pages in the book to learn about a subject.

You might also use the Internet. Web pages have **menus and icons**. Readers click on an icon, or picture. They can read more information. If they click on a menu, it drops down a list of choices.

Click on the icon for "Games in America." A menu opens. It shows the kinds of games played in America. Click on "Playground Games." Then more information will show on the screen.

Guided Practice

Read the questions. Then answer them.

Which of these would you use to find out more about owls?

A The Big Book of Mammals

B The Book of Birds

C The Adventures of the Owl and the Pussycat

D www.reptilesoftheworld.com

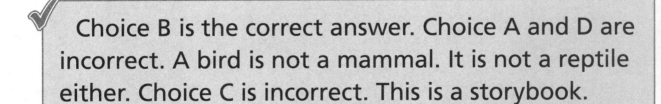

Choice B is the correct answer. Choice A and D are incorrect. A bird is not a mammal. It is not a reptile either. Choice C is incorrect. This is a storybook.

Which would be the <u>best</u> place to check if a book has facts about what an owl eats?

A title page

B book cover

C index

D headings

Choice C is the correct answer. The index lists the topics in a book. Choices A, B, and D are incorrect. The title page tells the name of the book. The book cover tells the title, too. The headings may tell what is in the chapter. You would have to look at every heading in the book. Looking at the index is a quicker way to find out.

Be careful with your fact-finding. Books, magazines, and newspapers are good places to look for facts. Websites can be, too. You want to use a book or website that can be trusted. Be sure to check more than one place for your facts. Sometimes, information can be wrong. Or, the information is out of date. New findings mean that facts sometimes change. Or, the information might be someone's opinion. An opinion is not a fact. Facts can be proven. Opinions are what someone thinks.

A good fact finder thinks like a detective. Here are some questions to help you do this:

- What is the source of this fact?
- How old is the information?
- Who wrote the information?
- Why did they write it?
- Do other sources agree with this fact?

Notetaking

When you find your facts, you should write them down. This makes it easier to write your paper. If your teacher gave you a paper with questions, you can write your facts on the paper. You can also write your facts on a note card. Here are some tips on taking notes:

- write one fact
- use your own words
- tell where you found your facts

It is important to tell where you found your facts. Look at the **title page** of a book. This lists the name of the book and the author. Then look at the **copyright page.** This is the page after the title page. The copyright page tells who published the book and when it was published. Write down the title of the book and the author. Write down the page where you found the information.

Source {
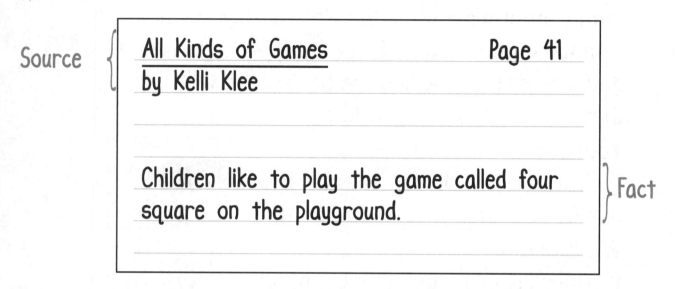

All Kinds of Games   Page 41
by Kelli Klee

Children like to play the game called four square on the playground.

} Fact

For a website, write the web address and the date you found the information.

Source {
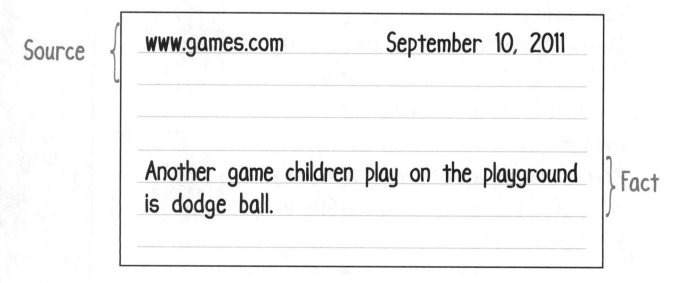

www.games.com   September 10, 2011

Another game children play on the playground is dodge ball.

} Fact

Read the passage. Then answer the questions.

The Days of the Week
By Kevin Thomas

The days of the week are named for gods and goddesses. The Norse people gave us the names for the days of the week. These people lived in the countries now called Norway, Sweden, Denmark, and Iceland. They believed in gods and goddesses. They named the days of the week after their Norse gods and goddesses.

Tuesday

Tyr was the god of war. Tuesday is named for him.

Wednesday

Wednesday is named after Odin, or Wodan. He was the god of war and wisdom. He carried a magic spear.

Thursday

Thursday is named for Thor. He is the god of thunder. He carried a magic hammer and wore a magic belt.

Friday

Friday is named for Freya. She is the goddess of love and beauty. She wore a magic necklace.

The Days of the Week   *57*

Fill in the note card with one fact from the
passage. Tell where you found the information.
Put the fact in your own words.

Taking good notes is important. You want to
record the fact to use in your paper. You also want
to know where you found your fact. This helps you
find it again if you need to go back to the source.
Here is a sample answer:

The Days of the Week   Page 57
by Kevin Thomas

Friday is named after the Norse goddess
named Freya.

Test Yourself

> **Index**
> **dog:** caring for, 8
> feeding, 10
> grooming, 12
> types of, 3

1 Which page would you read if you wanted to know how to care for a dog's fur?

A page 3

B page 8

C page 10

D page 12

2 Which of these is a good source of facts?

A poem

B play

C magazine

D story

3 Why should you use more than one source when researching a topic?

_____

_____

_____

_____

4 What information should you write on a note card?

_____

_____

_____

_____

Outlining the Research Paper

W.1.2, 5–8

Once you have your facts, then you are ready to plan your paper.

Step 3: Thesis Statement

You learned about the main idea in Lesson 3. The **thesis statement** is like the main idea. It tells the purpose of your paper.

The thesis statement is one sentence. It is not a fact. It is a sentence that tells the reader what you will talk about in your paper. The thesis statement belongs in the first paragraph.

Guided Practice

Read the questions. Then answer them.

Which of these <u>best</u> tells what the paper is about?

A My report is about summer.

B Summer means time spent on my grandfather's farm.

C I help feed the animals.

D I help pick the green beans.

Choice B is the correct answer. This paper is about summers spent on a farm. Choices A, C, and D are incorrect. Choice A is too general. Choices C and D are details about summers spent on the farm.

Why is a thesis statement important?

_____

_____

Every paper needs a thesis statement. The details in a paper support the thesis. Here is a sample answer:

The thesis statement tells what the paper is about. It tells what the reader will learn.

Step 4: Outline the Paper

The outline helps you plan your paper. First, write down the main questions to answer. Then write the facts that answer the question underneath. This helps you sort the facts into topics. Here is an example.

```
I.  What games do children play in
    America?
    A.  On the playground they play
        1. four square
        2. jump rope
        3. dodge ball

    B.  They play board games like
        1. Monopoly
        2. chess
        3. backgammon

    C.  They also play sports like
        1. football
        2. soccer
        3. races
```

Your paper will follow this map. You can then tell something about each game or sport. The last sentence is the conclusion. It tells the reader what they learned from your paper.

Here is an example:

American children play many different games.

Sometimes, the outline shows that you do not have enough facts. You may need to find more facts about a main idea. Or, you may have too many facts. Then you pick the most important facts and use only those.

Guided Practice

Read the outline. Then answer the questions.

I. Planting vegetables is good for you.

A. _____

   1. digging
   2. hoeing
   3. picking

B. _____

   1. vegetables
   2. fruits
   3. herbs

C. _____

   1. save money
   2. learn a skill
   3. fun

Match each main idea below with the facts about it
in the outline.

_____ You get other good things.

_____ You get exercise when you plant.

_____ You get fresh and good food from your
backyard.

✓ Details support a main idea. These main ideas
then support your thesis statement. Here are the
correct answers:

__C__ You get other good things.

__A__ You get exercise when you plant.

__B__ You get fresh and good food from your
backyard.

These facts can be matched to the main point
of the report. The outline would look like this:

I. Planting vegetables is good for you.
   A. You get exercise when you plant.
      1. digging
      2. hoeing
      3. picking

   B. You get fresh and good food
      from your backyard.
      1. vegetables
      2. fruits
      3. herbs

   C. You get other good things.
      1. save money
      2. learn a skill
      3. fun

Test Yourself

1 The thesis statement appears

  A at the end of the paper

  B in the index

  C in the first paragraph

  D in the title

2 How long should a thesis statement be?

  A one paragraph

  B one sentence

  C two paragraphs

  D three sentences

3 What is the purpose of an outline?

_____

_____

_____

_____

_____

Writing the Research Paper

W.1.2, 5–8

You have planned your paper. Now, you are ready to start writing.

Step 5: Write the Research Paper

You use the same steps as you did in other lessons. You have already planned your paper. Now, you write it. Then you revise and edit it. The last step is to publish it.

Visual aids are another way to give facts about a topic. You may want to use them in your paper.

Photographs and illustrations show what something looks like.

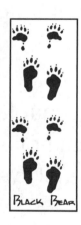

A **diagram** shows how something works. It also tells about something.

A **chart** compares things.

Black Bear
5 feet

Brown Bear
6 feet

Polar Bear
8 feet

A **map** shows where something is found.

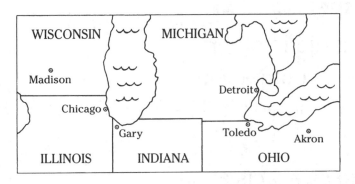

Step 6: Tell the Sources

Telling where you found your facts is a part of the research paper. You did this on your note cards. Now, you just have to list the sources at the end of the paper.

You tell the reader:

- where you found your facts (title)
- who created it (author and publisher)
- when they created it (year)

Here is an example of a source list. The writer only used books for his research.

Source List

Under the Sea by Carol Evans (New York:
    Universe Press, 2009)

Sea Worlds by Tommy Farrell (Washington, DC:
    Children's Press, 2010)

The Ocean by Helen O'Connor (New York:
    Nature Press, 2011)

Guided Practice

Read the questions. Then answer them.

What is the order used for the titles in the source list above?

A ABC order by book title

B ABC order by author's first name

C ABC order by author's last name

D ABC order by publisher's name

Choice C is the correct answer. The source list is organized in ABC order. It uses the author's last name to do this. Choices A, B, and D are incorrect.

Look at the source list on page 177. What is the name of the publisher of <u>The Ocean</u>?

_____

_____

 The publisher is given after the name of the city. The city tells where the publisher has its business. Here is the correct answer:

Nature Press

Publishing the Paper

You can publish your paper in different ways. You could give a copy to your teacher. You could make a slide show and show it to the class. Or, you could create a poster.

Test Yourself

1 You are writing about the ocean. What is one type of visual aid you could use in your report?

_____

_____

_____

_____

_____

2 Where would you find the source list in a report?

   A before the table of contents

   B on the copyright page

   C at the end of the paper

   D in the middle of the paper

3 What information about a book do you list in
a source list?

_____

_____

_____

_____

4 What does a diagram show?

_____

_____

_____

_____

Language Conventions

Good writing starts with good sentences. This unit looks at the rules that help you write clear sentences.

- **Lesson 13** covers punctuation and capitalization rules.

- **In Lesson 14,** you will review the rules of grammar. These rules help you to write clear sentences.

Language Conventions

W.1.5; L.1.1, 2

Here are some important rules to help you write better.

Punctuation Marks

A **sentence** is a whole thought. In a sentence, someone does something, or something happens.

A **period (.)** comes at the end of a telling sentence.

Today is Monday.

A **question mark (?)** comes at the end of an asking sentence.

Are you having fun?

An **exclamation point (!)** comes at the end of a sentence that shows surprise or strong feeling.

How nice you look!

Commas (,) are used in many ways. They are used in between the day and the year in a **date.** They are also used between the year and the rest of the sentence.

On July 14, 2009, my little brother was born.

Commas are used between words in a group.

Our flag is red, white, and blue.

Guided Practice

Read the sentence. Circle the correct end punctuation.

Do you like apples   .   ?

I painted a picture   .   ?

 An asking sentence ends with a question mark (?). A telling sentence ends with a period (.). Here are the correct answers:

Do you like apples   .   (?)

I painted a picture   (.)   ?

Which sentence shows the comma in the correct place?

A My birthday is June 14, 2001.

B My birthday, is June 14 2001.

C My birthday is June, 14 2001

D My, birthday is June 14 2001.

 Use a comma in a date. It goes after the day. It should be after the 14. Choice A is correct.

Capitalization

Capital letters are used to begin special words. The first word of a sentence begins with a capital letter.

She is reading a book.

The names of people, places, groups, days, months, holidays, and books begin with a capital letter.

Person: Dr. Gail Miller
Places: New York
Main Street
Day: Sunday
Month: June
Holiday: Thanksgiving
Book: The Cat in the Hat

Guided Practice

Read the question. Circle the best answer.

Which sentence shows the correct capital letters?

A My teacher is mrs. Chang.

B my teacher is mrs. chang.

C My teacher is Mrs. Chang.

D my teacher is Mrs. Chang.

The first letter in a sentence is always capital. So choices B and D are not correct. Names and titles are always capital. Choice C is the correct answer.

Prepositions

Prepositions show how a noun or pronoun is linked to another word in the sentence.

at	beyond	by	during	for	from
in	into	of	on	off	out
over	to	toward	under	with	

My brother is **in** the house.

I fell asleep **during** the movie.

His house is **beyond** the mailbox.

The car came **toward** us.

Adjectives

An **adjective** is a word that tells about a noun. It describes a person, an animal, a place, or a thing.

It may answer the question: What kind?

a **red** hen   **sunny** days

It may answer the questions: How many? How much?

three men   **ten** cups

An **article** is a special kind of adjective. It tells that a noun will follow. There are three articles: a, an, and the.

Place the article a before words that begin with a consonant sound.

There is **a** lion.

Place the article an before words that begin with a vowel sound.

There is **an** owl.

Demonstrative adjectives point out a noun. This and that point out a singular noun. These and those point out a plural noun.

This coat does not fit.
Those shoes fit the best.

Guided Practice

Circle the correct article.

She is looking for _____ apple.   a   an

Molly already has _____ ticket.   a   an

> The article <u>a</u> is used with words that start with a consonant sound. The article <u>an</u> is used before words that begin with a vowel sound. Here are the correct answers:

She is looking for _____ apple.   a   (an)

Molly already has _____ ticket.   (a)   an

Circle the correct adjective.

Michael does not want _____ book.   that   these

Dorrie wants to take _____ glasses.   this   those

> A singular noun uses <u>this</u> or <u>that</u>. <u>These</u> and <u>those</u> are used with a plural noun. Here are the correct answers:

Michael does not want _____ book.   (that)   these

Dorrie wants to take _____ glasses.   this   (those)

© The Continental Press, Inc.   DUPLICATING THIS MATERIAL IS ILLEGAL.

Test Yourself

1 Which sentence should end with a period?

   A Can you come here

   B Did you eat your dinner

   C The peas tasted good

   D When will you be finished

2 Which sentence shows the correct capital letters?

   A Pedro will come on june 8.

   B Pedro will come on June 8.

   C pedro will come on june 8.

   D pedro will come on June 8.

3 Which sentence shows the commas in the correct places?

   A I saw a bird, a dog, and a cat.

   B I saw, a bird, a dog and, a cat.

   C I saw a bird, a dog and, a cat.

   D I, saw a bird a dog, and a cat.

Rewrite the sentence. Correct the mistakes.

4 the women were shopping at lincoln Mall?

_____

_____

_____

_____

_____

Write an asking sentence.

5 _____

_____

_____

_____

Complete the sentence by adding an adjective.

6 Shelly took her _____ coat
to the game.

LESSON

14

Grammar

W.1.5; L.1.1, 2

Nouns

Nouns are people, places, or things. Nouns can be singular. This means there is one. Nouns can be plural. This means there is more than one.

Singular:	cat	house	truck	box
Plural:	cats	houses	trucks	boxes

Add –s to most nouns to make them name more than one. Add –es to nouns that end in s, x, ch, or sh.

Sometimes you have to change a noun to mean more than one.

Singular: man   **Plural:** men

Singular: goose   **Plural:** geese

UNIT 4 ▓▓▓▓▓▓▓▓▓▓▓▓▓▓▓▓▓▓▓▓▓▓▓▓▓▓▓▓▓▓▓▓▓▓▓▓
Language Conventions

A **common noun** names something general. A
proper noun names something specific.

Common Noun	Proper Noun
friend	Lisa
country	United States of America
month	January
book	Alice in Wonderland

What do you notice about the proper nouns?
They always have capital letters.

A **possessive noun** tells who owns something.
You add an apostrophe and –s to show possession
or ownership.

Michael's hat   Zoe's purse

Pronouns

Use **pronouns** in place of nouns. They can be
subjects. They can also be objects.

Subjects: I   you   he   she   it   we   they
Objects: me   you   him   her   it   us   them

The pronoun is a subject here:

I think strawberries are good.

The pronoun is an object here:

Maya went skiing with **them.**

Possessive pronouns show ownership.

his jacket   **their** school   **my** teacher

Verbs

Verbs are action words. They tell what someone or something does or did. Verbs can tell about the past. They can tell about the present. They can tell about the future.

Past: We **walked** to school.
Present: We **walk** to school.
Future: We **will walk** to school.

Some verbs change when they talk about the past.

Present: They **run** a mile.
Past: They **ran** a mile.

A verb can be in plain form. Use plain form with nouns that name more than one.

Plain form: swim

The boys **swim** fast.

A verb can be in s-form. Use s-form with nouns that name one.

S-form: swims

Ella **swims** fast.

Guided Practice

Underline the noun in each sentence. Circle common or proper.

My brother is tall.   common   proper

China is far away.   common   proper

A proper noun names a specific thing, place, or person. A common noun does not. Here are the correct answers:

My <u>brother</u> is tall.   (common)   proper

<u>China</u> is far away.   common   (proper)

Read each sentence. Circle the correct noun.

Three _____ were white. house   houses

A _____ did a magic trick. clown   clowns

We each carried a _____. plate   plates

The noun should relate to the word that tells how many. Sometimes there are clue words that help you know. The articles <u>a</u> and <u>an</u> indicate one. Numbers often tell how many. Here are the correct answers:

Three _____ were white. house   (houses)

A _____ did a magic trick. (clown)   clowns

We each carried a _____. (plate)   plates

Read each sentence. Circle the letter of the sentence that uses a pronoun.

A Jim likes to skateboard.

B Ed will meet them at the park.

C Mrs. Taylor baked a pie.

D The store is closed.

The correct answer is choice B. <u>Them</u> is a pronoun. It is used in place of a noun. The noun would be the names of the people Ed will meet.

Read the sentence. Circle the letter of the sentence that talks about the past.

A She will pick some apples.

B She picks some apples

C She is picking some apples.

D She picked some apples.

 You can add –ed to a verb. This makes it in the past. The correct answer is choice D.

Read each sentence. Circle the correct verb.

The dogs _____ across the yard. race   races

Peter _____ over the line.   jump   jumps

The chickens _____ in the barn.   live   lives

The noun and verb should always agree. A noun that means more than one takes a plural verb. Use plain form. A noun that means only one takes a singular verb. Use s-form. Here are the correct answers:

The dogs _____ across the yard. (race)   races

Peter _____ over the line.   jump (jumps)

The chickens _____ in the barn.   (live)   lives

Test Yourself

1 Which sentence uses a proper noun?

A We ate at a restaurant.

B This book is very funny.

C My bike is over here.

D The game is at Liberty Stadium.

2 Which sentence uses a pronoun?

A Kevin is meeting Mike at the store.

B Shelly is going to Ann's house.

C Mrs. Smith gave Pat the cake.

D They went to the movies.

Edit this passage for mistakes. Write your corrections on the essay. Be sure to use the proofreading marks you know.

3   Baby tigers look like kitten. They are very small. Tigers like to ran and play. They get ready for hunting this way. They begin hunting at 6 months old. At 1 year, tigers hunts all their food. At 2 years, young Tigers leave their mothers. They are on their own!

Read the passage. Then answer the questions.

Dale City Elementary School to Have Art Classes

The elementary school in Dale City waited a long time for art classes. The city could not pay for these classes. But this year is different. The mayor said that the city has been given a gift. A former student of the school has given money for an arts program.

The students are excited about the new program. But there are still a few things to decide. What kinds of arts and crafts will the students learn? Will there be painting classes? Should the students learn pottery? Should they learn how to knit?

The principal of the school has asked the students. She wants to know what they would like to learn. Students can write letters telling what kind of art they want to do. The Dale City Elementary School Arts Program will be designed by the students themselves! Then the school will have a program they are sure to love. It's a great move for Dale City.

1 Read this question. Then plan, write, revise, and edit your answer on the pages that follow.

> Imagine you go to Dale City Elementary School. What will you choose to learn in the arts program? Write a letter to the principal of the school. Tell her your opinion about the arts program you would like to have. Be sure to:
>
> - include an opening sentence that gives your opinion about the arts program. Make sure you tell what you would like to learn.
>
> - write supporting sentences that back up your opinion. Use facts from the article. Also, use facts from your own experience.

Practice Test

Prewriting

Underline or mark up the question as you wish.
Then use the rest of the page to plan your answer.
Choose a graphic organizer to plan your answer.

_____

_____

_____

_____

_____

_____

_____

_____

_____

_____

_____

Prewriting

Drafting

Use this page to write your draft.

_____

_____

_____

_____

_____

_____

_____

_____

_____

_____

_____

Revising and Editing

Use this page to make your revisions. Then edit your work.

_____

_____

_____

_____

_____

_____

_____

_____

_____

_____

_____

Publishing

Write your final copy on the page below. Then show it to your teacher.

_____

_____

_____

_____

_____

_____

_____

_____

_____

_____

2

The Forest

The forest is has tall trees The leaves have many colors. They changes over the year. In Winter, there are no leaves on most of the trees. In spring, new leaves grow. In summer, the leaves get bigger. In fall, some leaves turn color and fall off. some trees have green leaves all year.

There are other plants in the forest. A fern look like a green feather? It grows under trees. Moss like looks like a rug on the forest floor. It is soft, thick plants.

HANDBOOK

Using Capital Letters

- Begin every sentence with a capital letter: **M**y bike is green.

- Begin each part of a person's name with a capital letter. Include titles that are used as part of the name.

    Ryan **W. C**ooper   **A**unt **R**osa

    President **A**dams   **D**r. **C**hen

- Begin words that name days, months, holidays, and places with a capital letter.

    Monday   **O**ctober   **F**lag **D**ay

    Riverside **S**chool   **N**ew **Y**ork **C**ity

- Do NOT begin the names of seasons with a capital letter.

    winter   fall   spring   summer

Using Punctuation Marks
End Marks

- End every sentence with a period (**.**), a question mark (**?**), or an exclamation point (**!**).

- End a statement with a period: Tadpoles turn into frogs**.**

- End a question with a question mark: Where is your jacket**?**

- End an exclamation with an exclamation point: I love summer**!**

Commas (,)

- Use commas between words that name things in a group.

    Mix together the flour**,** sugar**,** salt**,** and oil.

- Use a comma between the day and year in a date.

    April 7, 2011

- Use a comma between a city and state.

    Omaha**,** Nebraska

Apostrophes (')

- Use an apostrophe to show who owns or has something. If the owner is singular (one person or thing), add an apostrophe and -s.

    Matt**'s** dad   a duck**'s** beak

- If the owner is plural (more than one) and ends in -s, add just an apostrophe.

    three girl**s'** scores   all the cat**s'** tails

Using Correct Grammar
Subject-Verb Agreement

- When you use an action verb in the present tense, add -s or -es to the verb if the subject is a singular noun (one person or thing). Do not add -s or -es to the verb if the subject is plural (more than one).

    Emily sing**s**   children sing   Carlos and Becky sing

- If the subject is a pronoun, add -s or -es to the verb only if the pronoun is he, she, or it.

    he eat**s**   I eat   you eat   we eat   they eat

Proofreading Symbols

Symbol	Meaning	Example
∧	Add letters or words.	Our flag now has 50 stars.
⊙	Add a period.	We salute our flag⊙
≡	Capitalize a letter.	The <u>u</u>nited <u>s</u>tates flag has changed.
∧	Add a comma.	Our country's flag is red, white, and blue.
⌐	Delete letters or words.	The flag has 13 ~~stripes~~ stripes.
∿	Switch the position of letters or words.	One was star added for each state.

Notes